D0853239

COOKING
FOR TWO

CHARMAINE SOLOMON

HAMLYN

Published 1993 by Hamlyn
an imprint of the Octopus Publishing Group,
a division of Reed International Books Australia Pty Ltd
22 Salmon Street, Port Melbourne, Victoria 3207

Designed by Louise Lavarack
Photographs by Michael Cook
Styling by Margaret Alcock
Food cooked by Jill Pavey, Nina Harris, Virginia McLeod
China: White china from The Bay Tree Kitchen Shop, Woollahra, NSW
Ceramic bowls from Made in Japan, Neutral Bay, NSW
Typeset in 9½ on 12pt Berkeley Old Style Book by Midland Typesetters
Produced in Hong Kong by Mandarin Offset

National Library of Australia
   cataloguing-in-publication data:

Solomon, Charmaine.
   Cooking for two.
   Includes index.
   ISBN 0 947334 45 9.

   1. Cookery for two. 2. Cookery, Oriental. I. Title. (Series: Solomon,
   Charmaine. Asian cooking library).

641.561

INTRODUCTION

The best thing about cooking for two is that meals don't take as long to prepare because there is less to slice, dice, chop or grate. On the other hand a simmered or braised dish takes just as long to cook for two as for six. If time is something you are short of, consider making double quantities of long-cooked dishes that freeze well. In a stir-fried dish, however, the small quantities are a positive advantage as they sizzle to tender perfection in less than five minutes.

One of the drawbacks of cooking for two, however, is that even the smallest sizes of canned foods are often far more than is needed. So what do you do with the rest of a can of water chestnuts or bamboo shoots? You can refrigerate them, changing the water every day and they should last for a week or so. These particular items don't freeze well.

Leftover coconut milk, though, is a different matter. It quickly turns rancid, so pour the remaining coconut milk into an ice-cube tray and freeze it without delay. When it is frozen solid, pop the cubes into a freezer bag. You now have coconut milk in convenient quantities to enrich a curry or soup. Most cubes hold about a tablespoon.

Buy spices in small quantities, store them in airtight glass jars in a cool, dark place and use them within six months or so. Or store them in the freezer and they will keep practically for ever.

Soups

Most of these soups are light and ideal as a starter to a meal. Some, served with rice or noodles, can be eaten as a light main meal.

A fragrant soup stock with delicate Asian flavours used as a clear broth on its own or as a basis for other soups. Strain and use it immediately, or cool and chill, removing any fat from the surface and freezing for use at another time. Since good stock takes a while to cook, it is one of those things worth making in larger quantities, then freezing in amounts of 2 to 3 cups.

Soup Stock

- 6 cups water
- 1 large onion
- 1 large carrot
- 5 thin slices fresh ginger
- 5 fresh coriander roots with stems
- a few celery leaves
- 500 g (1 lb) chicken necks and backs
  or substitute beef or pork bones
- 1 teaspoon salt
- ½ teaspoon whole black peppercorns

Bring water to boil in a large saucepan. Meanwhile peel and quarter onion; scrape carrot. Add to saucepan with remaining ingredients. Return to boil, then lower heat. Cover and simmer for 45 minutes to 1 hour.

If you are apprehensive about the chilli in Thai soups, try this one which is fragrant and mild. A small amount of rice vermicelli or quick-cooking egg noodles can turn this into a light meal.

THAI SOUP WITH STUFFED MUSHROOMS

- 6 medium dried shiitake (Chinese) mushrooms
- 1 spring onion, including some green
- 60 g (2 oz) minced pork or chopped raw prawns
- ½ teaspoon finely chopped garlic
- 2 teaspoons finely chopped coriander leaves
- 2 teaspoons Maggi Seasoning
- ground black pepper to taste
- 2 teaspoons finely chopped water chestnuts
- 3 cups chicken stock, fat removed
- ¼ medium green cucumber
- 2 teaspoons fish sauce, or to taste

Pour very hot water over mushrooms in a bowl and leave to soak for 30 minutes. Drain, squeeze out excess water; cut off and discard stems. Cut several diagonal slices from spring onion and set aside, covered. Finely chop remainder. Combine pork or prawns with garlic, finely chopped spring onion, coriander, Maggi Seasoning, pepper and water chestnuts. Mix well. Pack mixture into drained mushroom caps and cook for about 15 minutes in 1½ cups of stock. (It is important to cook in only a small amount of stock so that the filling remains intact in the mushrooms until cooked.) Peel cucumber; cut in halves lengthwise, scoop out seeds and cut cucumber across into thin slices.

Add remaining stock, fish sauce and cucumber slices to saucepan and simmer for 3 to 4 minutes. Place 3 mushrooms in each soup plate and ladle soup over mushrooms. Garnish with reserved spring onion slices.

Chicken Soup with Cucumber Slices

- *half a green cucumber*
- *2 cups chicken stock*
- *¼ cup diced cooked chicken*
- *1 tablespoon finely chopped coriander leaves*
- *½ teaspoon sesame oil*

Peel cucumber; cut in halves lengthwise and scoop out seeds with a small spoon. Cut across into thin slices. In a saucepan bring stock to boil. Add cucumber and cook for about 3 minutes, so that cucumber is tender but crisp. Add chicken and heat through. Stir in coriander and sesame oil and serve.

Make a meal of this South Indian soup with steamed rice.

PRAWN AND LENTIL SOUP

- 125 g (4 oz) green beans
- ⅓ cup red lentils
- 250 g (8 oz) small prawns, shelled and deveined
- 1 tablespoon oil
- 1 medium onion, finely sliced
- 1 small clove garlic, finely chopped
- ½ teaspoon grated fresh ginger
- 1 fresh red chilli, split in half and seeded
- ½ teaspoon ground turmeric
- salt to taste
- ¼ cup canned coconut milk
- lemon juice to taste

Trim beans, string if necessary, and cut into thin diagonal slices. Wash lentils thoroughly; drain.

Heat oil in a saucepan and fry onion over high heat, stirring constantly, until golden brown. Stir in garlic and ginger, then add chilli halves and turmeric; fry for a few seconds more. Add lentils and fry, stirring, for about 2 minutes. Add 2 cups water and bring to boil, stirring occasionally. Reduce heat, cover and cook for 15 minutes. Add prawns, beans and salt. Cook until lentils are soft. Add coconut milk mixed with ¼ cup water. Stir in lemon juice.

Here's a tip to save time and effort. Instead of soaking, slicing and cooking only 2 dried mushrooms, do 8 or 10—it takes the same time. Just increase the amount of soaking liquid, soy sauce and sugar. Set aside for stir-fried dishes.

CHICKEN AND BEAN CURD SOUP

- 2 dried shiitake (Chinese) mushrooms
- 2 teaspoons soy sauce
- ½ teaspoon sugar
- 1 chicken breast fillet
- 1 square fresh bean curd
- 2 cups chicken stock
- 1 spring onion, finely sliced
- few drops sesame oil

Soak mushrooms in hot water for 30 minutes; cut off stems and discard. Reserve soaking water. Cut caps across in thin slices; put in a small pan with ¼ cup of soaking water, the soy sauce and sugar. Bring to boil and cook until almost all liquid has evaporated.

Cut chicken fillet into small dice. Slice bean curd square into 3 strips, then across to make equal-sized dice. Bring chicken stock to boil, add chicken and simmer for 1 minute. Add mushrooms and bean curd and bring back to a simmer. Add spring onion and sesame oil. Remove from heat and cover. Leave to stand for 1 minute, then serve.

Soup with Vegetables

- 3 cups chicken stock
- 12 small sprigs broccoli
- 60 g (2 oz) snow peas or sugar snap peas
- 2 tablespoons finely chopped coriander leaves
- few drops sesame oil

Bring chicken stock to boil. Add broccoli and cook for about 4 minutes. Add peas and cook 2 minutes more. Remove from heat. Stir in coriander and sesame oil and serve immediately.

This Chinese soup takes its name from the fact that the beaten egg looks like chrysanthemum petals when poured into boiling stock.

Egg Flower Soup

- 2 cups chicken stock
- 1 tablespoon dry sherry
- ½ teaspoon sesame oil
- salt to taste
- 1 egg, beaten
- 1 spring onion finely sliced

Bring stock to boil. Add sherry, sesame oil, and salt if necessary. Slowly pour beaten egg into boiling stock. Stir once or twice. Serve immediately, sprinkled with spring onion.

SEAFOOD

The fresh herb and coconut chutney so popular in India as an accompaniment to rice and lentil pancakes is used in this recipe as a stuffing for fish. I tasted it in both Bombay and Goa, once in a delicate pomfret which was crisply fried, and once in a robust mackerel which was grilled. Try and persuade the fishmonger to bone the fish for you, but if you get stuck with the task, a very sharp filleting knife is the answer.

FISH WITH GREEN CHUTNEY

- 2 small whole fish, about 375 g (12 oz) each
- coarse salt

GREEN CHUTNEY
- ½ cup fresh grated or desiccated coconut
- ⅓ cup chopped fresh coriander
- 1 small onion, chopped
- 1 teaspoon chopped garlic
- pinch of ground cummin
- 3 large green chillies, seeded and chopped
- 1 teaspoon lemon juice
- ¼ teaspoon sugar
- salt to taste
- lime wedges

Purchase fish scaled and cleaned. Rub out cavity with coarse salt; rinse well. With a sharp knife separate flesh from bones and lift out bones to make a pocket for green chutney. Score fish three or four times on each side. Rub salt over fish.

GREEN CHUTNEY If desiccated coconut is used, sprinkle with a little water and mix lightly with fingertips to moisten coconut evenly. Put all ingredients into an electric blender and blend to smooth, thick paste. If necessary add a little water to help blending.

Fill fish cavity with Green Chutney and grill fish over coals or under a pre-heated griller, turning once, until flesh is opaque and tender when pierced at its thickest point. Or, if preferred, dip fish in seasoned flour and shallow fry in hot oil until golden brown. Garnish with wedges of lime and serve with hot steamed rice.

STEAMED FISH WITH GINGER

- 60 g (2 oz) fresh young ginger root
- juice of ½ lemon
- 1 tablespoon peanut oil
- 2 teaspoons sesame oil
- 3 cloves garlic, finely sliced
- 1½ tablespoons sesame seeds
- 1 tablespoon dark soy sauce
- 375 g (12 oz) fish cutlets or steaks

Scrape skin from ginger and slice very thinly. Cut slices into fine, thread-like slivers. Marinate with lemon juice in a bowl.

Meanwhile prepare remaining ingredients. Heat oils together in a small frying pan and fry garlic over low heat, stirring frequently, until just golden. Do not let it burn. Pour oil and garlic slices over ginger. In same pan dry-fry the sesame seeds, stirring until golden brown. Stir into ginger mixture. Add soy sauce and mix well. Place fish cutlets on individual sheets of foil large enough to enclose fish. Sprinkle ginger mixture over cutlets. Seal foil and place packets in a steamer. Steam for 15 minutes. Serve with steamed rice and accompaniments of choice.

INDIAN FISH CURRY WITH COCONUT

- 2 fish cutlets
- lemon juice
- salt
- 2 large dried red chillies
- 2 teaspoons desiccated coconut
- 1 teaspoon ground coriander
- ½ teaspoon ground cummin
- 1 clove garlic, finely chopped
- ½ teaspoon finely chopped fresh ginger
- 1 teaspoon tamarind pulp
- 2 teaspoons ghee or oil
- 1 small onion, finely chopped
- ¼ cup canned coconut milk
- salt to taste

Wash fish, rub with lemon juice and salt; set aside. Soak chillies in hot water for 10 minutes. In a dry pan toast coconut, stirring constantly, until brown. Remove coconut to a plate and toast coriander and cummin in same pan over low heat, stirring constantly, and taking care that they do not burn. Remove chillies from water and place with coconut, spices, garlic and ginger into a blender and blend to a smooth paste, adding a little water if necessary. Soak tamarind in ⅓ cup hot water, squeezing to dissolve; strain. Heat ghee or oil in a heavy pan and fry onion, stirring frequently, until soft. Add blended mixture and fry over medium heat, stirring until it darkens and smells aromatic. Add coconut milk, salt and tamarind liquid. Bring slowly to simmering point, stirring to prevent mixture curdling. Add fish and simmer gently, uncovered, until cooked. Serve with rice.

THAI-STYLE FRIED FISH

- *2 tablespoons peanut oil*
- *375 g (12 oz) fish fillets*
- *3 spring onions, cut into 2.5 cm (1 inch) pieces*
- *2 cloves garlic, crushed*
- *1 teaspoon finely grated fresh ginger*
- *1 tablespoon light soy sauce*
- *2 teaspoons palm sugar or brown sugar*
- *2 teaspoons lemon juice*
- *2 teaspoons fish sauce*
- *ground black pepper to taste*
- *1 tablespoon finely chopped fresh coriander leaves*
- *½ fresh red chilli, seeded and sliced*

Heat oil in a pan and fry fish in hot oil first on one side and then on the other until lightly browned and cooked through—flesh will become opaque. Transfer fish to serving platter and keep warm. Let pan cool slightly, then add spring onions, garlic and ginger. Cook over low heat, stirring, until soft and golden. Mix soy sauce, sugar, lemon juice, fish sauce and pepper in a small bowl. Stir into pan and simmer for 1 minute. Pour sauce over fish, garnish with coriander leaves and sliced chilli and serve immediately with steamed rice.

This recipe will give you more curry paste than you need for one curry, but the curry paste is not worth making in tiny amounts. It keeps well if stored in a clean, dry, tightly stoppered bottle and refrigerated. Or you can divide it into tablespoon-size portions and freeze.

THAI PRAWN CURRY

- *375 g (12 oz) raw prawns*
- *½ cup canned coconut milk (see Note)*
- *1 tablespoon Thai Red Curry Paste (see below)*
- *2 teaspoons fish sauce*
- *1 fresh red chilli, seeded*

1 teaspoon palm sugar or brown sugar

2 kaffir lime leaves

few small basil leaves

THAI RED CURRY PASTE
- *4 to 6 dried red chillies*
- *2 small brown onions, chopped*
- *1 teaspoon black peppercorns*
- *2 teaspoons ground cummin*
- *1 tablespoon ground coriander*
- *2 tablespoons chopped fresh coriander, including root*
- *1 teaspoon salt*
- *1 stem lemon grass, finely sliced,*

or 2 teaspoons chopped lemon rind

- *2 teaspoons chopped galangal root in brine*
  - *1 tablespoon chopped garlic*
  - *2 teaspoons dried shrimp paste*
    - *1 tablespoon oil*
    - *1 teaspoon turmeric*
  - *2 teaspoons paprika (see Note)*

Shell and devein prawns, reserving heads. Discard hard top shell from prawn heads and wash heads thoroughly. Put coconut milk in a wok and heat to boiling. Add Curry Paste and fry, stirring constantly, until thick and oily. Stir in ½ cup water, fish sauce, chilli, palm sugar and lime leaves. Bring slowly to a simmer, stirring. Add prawn heads and cook, uncovered, stirring frequently, on low heat until heads are cooked and flavours mellow—about 15 minutes. (The prawn heads are edible and have a wonderful flavour.) Add shelled prawns and cook for 5 minutes more or until prawns change colour and flesh becomes opaque. Sprinkle with basil leaves and serve hot with white rice.

THAI RED CURRY PASTE Remove stems from chillies. If you want the curry to be as hot as it is in Thailand, leave seeds in, otherwise shake them out. Break chillies into pieces and soak in just enough hot water to cover for 10 minutes. Place in an electric blender container with all other ingredients. Blend until a smooth paste forms, stopping frequently to push ingredients down with a spatula. You may need to add a little water to assist the blending.

Note Even though paprika is not used in Thailand, I have added it to give this curry the requisite red colour without using as many red chillies as would be used on its home ground.

Canned coconut milks vary a lot in thickness, and this recipe is based on a rich, thick coconut milk. If you open the can and find it is thin and watery, simply use a whole cup of coconut milk and omit or reduce the amount of water.

It sounds as if it may be hot, but this dish is red from tomatoes not chillies.

THAI FISH IN RED SAUCE

- *2 tablespoons oil*
- *1 onion, finely chopped*
- *2 ripe tomatoes, peeled and chopped*
- *1 tablespoon vinegar*
- *salt and pepper to taste*
- *1 fresh red chilli, seeded and chopped*
- *375 g (12 oz) fish fillets*
- *2 tablespoons chopped fresh coriander leaves*

Heat oil in a pan and fry onion over moderate heat until soft and golden brown. Add tomatoes, vinegar, salt, pepper and chilli. Cover pan and simmer for 20 minutes, or until tomatoes form a pulp and sauce is thick. Add fish fillets, spooning some of the sauce over. Cover and cook until fish is done—the flesh will be opaque. The fish will be ready in only a short cooking time, so be careful not to overcook. Serve hot with steamed rice and garnished with coriander leaves.

Trout with a Far Eastern flavour is more interesting than most ways of cooking this popular fish.

FRIED TROUT WITH GINGER

- 2 small trout, cleaned
- ½ teaspoon salt
- ½ teaspoon five spice powder
- cornflour to coat
- ¼ cup peanut oil
- 1 spring onion, sliced
- 1 tablespoon very finely shredded ginger
- 1 tablespoon chopped fresh coriander

SAUCE
- 1 tablespoon red wine vinegar
- 1 tablespoon dry sherry
- 1½ tablespoons light soy sauce
- 1 teaspoon sugar
- 1 teaspoon sesame oil

Mix sauce ingredients together in a small bowl and set aside.

Rub trout cavity with damp paper towel dipped in salt. Make shallow diagonal cuts on each side of fish and rub in a mixture of salt and five spice powder. Roll fish in cornflour to coat, shaking off excess. Heat peanut oil in a heavy frying pan or wok and fry spring onion and ginger for only a few seconds. Remove with a frying spatula and set aside. Place fish in pan and fry until golden brown underneath; turn over, lower heat, and fry until other side is browned and fish is cooked through—the flesh will be opaque.

Pour off as much oil as possible, then pour sauce mixture over fish. Return spring onion and ginger to pan. Raise heat and cook until sauce boils—about 1 minute. Lift fish to a warm serving platter, spoon sauce over and serve garnished with coriander.

PRAWN OR CRAB OMELETTE

- *4 eggs*
- *salt to taste*
- *pinch black pepper*
- *125 g (4 oz) cooked prawns or 1 small cooked crab*
- *oil for frying*
- *1 spring onion, chopped*

Beat eggs slightly and season with salt and pepper. Shell, devein and chop prawns, or pick flesh from crab. Heat 2 teaspoons oil in a frying pan and sauté spring onion for 1 minute. Remove mixture to a small plate and mix with prawns or crab.

Heat 1 teaspoon oil, pour in half of beaten eggs and cook, drawing egg mixture in from sides of pan until set on bottom and creamy on top. Spoon half of shellfish mixture down centre of omelette and fold omelette over to enclose filling. Transfer to a warm serving plate. Repeat with remaining beaten egg and filling. Serve with salad.

Steamed Fish Balls with Sugar Peas

- 375 g (12 oz) fillets of fish
- ½ teaspoon finely grated fresh ginger
- 1 clove garlic, crushed
- ½ teaspoon salt or to taste
- 1 egg yolk
- 2 teaspoons cornflour
- sesame oil
- 1 tablespoon peanut oil
- 125 g (4 oz) sugar snap or snow peas, strings removed
- ½ cup fish or chicken stock
- 1 tablespoon oyster sauce
- ½ teaspoon sugar

Remove skin and any bones from fish and chop very finely (a food processor is useful for this). Mix with ginger, garlic, salt, egg yolk and 1 teaspoon of cornflour. Lightly grease hands with sesame oil and form fish into small balls about 2.5 cm (1 inch) across. Place balls on a plate; put plate on a rack and steam in a covered pan over gently boiling water for 10 minutes. Meanwhile mix remaining cornflour with 1 tablespoon cold water.

When fish balls are cooked, heat peanut oil in a wok and toss sugar peas in oil until they turn bright green—about 1½ minutes. Push peas to side of wok, pour in stock, add cornflour mixture and cook, stirring, until thickened and clear—about 1 minute. Stir in oyster sauce and sugar; toss to coat sugar peas.

Arrange fish balls on warm serving dish and spoon sugar peas and sauce over. Serve immediately.

Fillets of Fish in Black Bean Sauce

- *375 g (12 oz) fillets of firm white fish*
- *cornflour*
- *2 tablespoons canned salted black beans*
- *2 cloves garlic*
- *1 teaspoon sugar*
- *1 teaspoon finely grated fresh ginger*
- *2 tablespoons dry sherry*
- *peanut oil*
- *2 spring onions, cut in thin diagonal slices*

Cut fillets in halves lengthwise, then cut each piece across into finger-size pieces. Dust with 1 tablespoon of cornflour. Put black beans in a sieve and rinse under cold water. Transfer to a wooden board and chop or mash with a fork. Crush garlic with sugar and mix together with beans and ginger. Mix sherry and 2 teaspoons of cornflour into ½ cup water.

Heat wok; add 3 tablespoons peanut oil and when hot put in pieces of fish, a few at a time, fry for 1 minute or until colour changes. Drain with slotted spoon and transfer to a plate lined with paper towel. When all pieces are cooked, drain excess oil from wok and wipe wok dry. Add 2 teaspoons oil to wok and fry black bean mixture, stirring, for 1 minute. Add sherry mixture and stir constantly until it boils and thickens slightly. Add fish pieces and spring onions. Heat through and serve with steamed rice.

This Cambodian dish is intensely flavoured. Don't be daunted by the amount of garlic!

FISH WITH COCONUT CREAM

- *375 g (12 oz) fish fillets*
- *1 large dry chilli*
- *10 cloves garlic*
- *2 kaffir lime leaves*
- *1 slice fresh galangal or 1 teaspoon laos powder*
- *1 stalk lemon grass, finely sliced, or 1 strip lemon rind*
- *2 tablespoons peanut oil*
- *¾ cup canned coconut milk*
- *1 tablespoon fish sauce*
- *1 tablespoon chopped roasted peanuts*
- *3 small dried chillies*
- *oil for frying*
- *sprigs of fresh basil*

Wash fillets and slice into serving pieces. Remove stalk and seeds from large chilli and soak in hot water for 10 minutes. Pound chilli, garlic, lime leaves, galangal, and lemon grass to a paste. (You can make the paste in an electric blender, but you may need to add a tablespoon of oil to help blending.)

Heat oil in a wok or heavy frying pan and add prepared paste. Fry until cooked and fragrant, stirring constantly. Add pieces of fish and turn over carefully in mixture. Mix coconut milk with 1¼ cups water and add with fish sauce. Simmer over low heat for 10 minutes. Add peanuts just before end of cooking time. Meanwhile, fry chillies for a few seconds in a pan with a little hot oil. Garnish fish with chillies and basil and serve with hot cooked rice.

SQUID IN OYSTER SAUCE

- *300 g (10 oz) cleaned squid*
- *12 snow peas*
- *1 tablespoon peanut oil*
- *½ teaspoon finely grated fresh ginger*
- *½ cup fish or chicken stock*
- *1 teaspoon light soy sauce*
- *2 teaspoons oyster sauce*
- *2 teaspoons cornflour*

Slit body of squid lengthwise. Rinse well and on inner surface make shallow slits with a sharp knife to form a pattern of diamond shapes. Holding knife at a 45° angle gives a good appearance and exposes more surface area. Cut squid into pieces. String snow peas.

Heat peanut oil in wok and add ginger and squid pieces; stir-fry, tossing constantly, for 2 to 3 minutes. Lift out with slotted spoon onto a plate. Add snow peas to wok and toss for a few seconds. Stir in stock, soy and oyster sauces. Bring to boil. Mix cornflour with 2 tablespoons cold water and stir into sauce. Return squid to wok and heat through, then serve at once.

The fish for this dish can be prepared up to a day ahead. If you cook to the point where the pieces are boiled and drained, only a few minutes are needed to prepare the sauce and assemble the dish.

VELVET FISH WITH OYSTER SAUCE

- 375 g (12 oz) fillet of snapper or similar fish
- salt to taste
- pinch pepper
- 2 teaspoons cornflour
- 3 tablespoons peanut oil
- 1 tablespoon egg white
- ½ teaspoon finely grated fresh ginger
- 4 spring onions, cut into bite-size pieces
- 2 tablespoons oyster sauce

Skin fillet; remove any bones and cut into bite-size pieces. Season with salt and pepper and set aside in a bowl for 10 minutes. Sprinkle with cornflour and 1 tablespoon of oil. Mix well until fish pieces are coated. Leave for 15 minutes. Add egg white and mix in. Chill for a further 30 minutes.

Bring about 5 cups of water to boil, adding 1 tablespoon of peanut oil. Drop in fish pieces (making sure they don't stick together). Return to boil and cook for 1 minute. Lift out with a large, shallow sieve and drain.

Heat a wok; add remaining tablespoon of oil and swirl to coat inside of wok. Add ginger and spring onions; stir-fry on high heat for 1 minute. Stir in oyster sauce mixed with 2 tablespoons water. Add fish pieces and heat through. Serve immediately.

Braised Fish and Prawn Rolls

- *8 raw prawns*
- *375 g (12 oz) firm white fish fillets*
- *2 tablespoons peanut oil*
- *3 thin slices fresh ginger*
- *1 tablespoon light soy sauce*
- *1 tablespoon dry sherry*
- *2 spring onions, sliced finely*

Shell and devein prawns. Remove skin and any bones from fish fillets and cut into 8 strips, each large enough to roll round a prawn. Fasten with wooden toothpicks. Heat oil in wok; add slices of ginger and fry until golden. Add fish rolls and fry for 2 minutes, turning carefully with tongs.

Drain excess oil from wok. Add ¼ cup hot water with soy sauce and sherry. Cover and simmer for 2 minutes or until fish is opaque. Transfer fish rolls to serving dish. Discard slices of ginger and remove toothpicks. Add spring onions to wok and stir until bright green. Pour sauce over fish.

SZECHWAN-STYLE STEAMED FISH

- 1 whole fish, about 750 g (1½ lb)
- ½ teaspoon salt
- ½ teaspoon finely grated fresh ginger
- 1 tablespoon dry sherry
- 1 tablespoon peanut oil
- 1 teaspoon sesame oil
- 1 teaspoon crushed garlic
- 1 teaspoon finely chopped fresh ginger
- 2 teaspoons chilli bean sauce
- 2 spring onions, finely sliced
- 2 tablespoons chopped fresh coriander leaves

Purchase fish cleaned and scaled. Slash diagonally. Rub over with salt and grated ginger. Place in a lightly oiled heatproof dish and steam over boiling water for 8 to 10 minutes. Pour off liquid that collects around fish into a measuring cup. Add sherry. Heat peanut and sesame oils in a wok or heavy pan. Add garlic and ginger and stir-fry for 1 minute. Add bean sauce, sherry mixture and spring onions; bring to boil. Pour over fish and garnish with coriander. Serve with rice.

CHICKEN

Kashmiri-grown apricots are small and are traditionally dried whole with the seed—they have a wonderful flavour. If you can find them, use them, otherwise use the Australian dried apricots, which have more flavour than those from the Middle East.

KASHMIRI CHICKEN WITH APRICOTS

- 1 tablespoon ghee or oil
- 1 fresh green chilli, seeded and chopped
- ½ teaspoon finely grated fresh ginger
- 1 small clove garlic, finely chopped
- 1 large onion, finely sliced
- 1 cardamom pod, bruised
- small piece cinnamon stick
- 500 g (1 lb) chicken pieces—thighs, drumsticks or breast
- 1 small ripe tomato, chopped
- salt to taste
- ¼ teaspoon saffron strands
- 8 dried apricot halves

Heat ghee or oil in a heavy saucepan or flameproof casserole and fry chilli, ginger, garlic, onion, cardamom and cinnamon, stirring frequently, until onion is golden. Add chicken pieces and fry, turning them over in the mixture until colour changes. Stir in tomato, salt and ¼ cup hot water. Cover and simmer over low heat for 30 minutes.

Lightly toast saffron threads in a small pan, being careful

not to let them burn. Transfer to a bowl, crush with the back of a spoon and dissolve in 1 tablespoon boiling water. Add saffron and apricots to pan and stir. Cover and continue simmering for a further 10 minutes or until apricots are tender but not mushy and chicken is cooked. Serve with a pilau rice.

CHICKEN WITH LEMON GRASS

- *500 g (1 lb) chicken pieces*
- *2 stalks lemon grass, or thinly peeled rind of half a lemon*
- *2 spring onions*
- *salt to taste*
- *ground black pepper to taste*
- *1 tablespoon oil*
- *1 fresh red chilli, seeded and chopped*
- *1 teaspoon sugar*
- *¼ cup roasted peanuts, finely chopped*
- *1 tablespoon fish sauce*

Cut chicken into smaller serving pieces, chopping through bones with a cleaver. Remove outer leaves of lemon grass and finely slice tender white portion at base of stalks. Bruise with a mortar and pestle, or with handle of cleaver. (If using lemon peel, cut into very thin shreds with a sharp knife.) Finely slice spring onions, including the green part. Mix chicken pieces with lemon grass, spring onions, salt and pepper and set aside for 30 minutes.

Heat a wok, add oil and swirl to coat cooking surface. When oil is hot, add chicken mixture and stir-fry for 3 minutes. Add chilli and stir-fry over medium heat for 10 minutes more, or until chicken is no longer pink. Season with sugar and some extra black pepper; add peanuts. Stir well. Add fish sauce and toss. Serve with plain rice or noodles.

In India this dish is traditionally cooked over coals in a clay oven called a tandoor, in which food cooks very quickly due to the intense heat. You can adapt the recipe for a barbecue, grill or oven. If you decide to use the barbecue or grill, the chicken must be cut in halves lengthwise. For the barbecue, allow the fire to burn down so that the chicken cooks over glowing coals. Place the chicken halves on a rack above the coals and cook until tender, turning the pieces so they cook on both sides. Baste with melted ghee if the chicken looks dry.

TANDOORI CHICKEN

- 1 spring chicken, about 800 g (1¼ lbs)
- ⅓ cup plain yoghurt
- salt to taste
- 1 small clove garlic, crushed
- 1 teaspoon finely grated fresh ginger
- ¼ teaspoon white pepper
- ¼ teaspoon chilli powder
- ½ teaspoon garam masala
- red food colour, optional
- 1 tablespoon ghee

Remove skin from chicken and make slits in the flesh to allow marinade to penetrate. Combine yoghurt with all other ingredients except ghee. Rub this marinade over and inside chicken. Set aside for 2 to 4 hours or cover and refrigerate overnight. (Traditionally, tandoori foods are coloured a bright orange-red. I prefer not to use colouring, but you can add a quantity of paprika to the marinade if you want this colour.)

Preheat the oven to 200°C (400°F). Melt ghee in a roasting pan and place chicken in pan breast down. Spoon melted ghee over and roast for 20 minutes. Turn chicken onto one side and roast for another 15 minutes. Turn onto the other side, baste again and roast for a further 15 minutes. For the final 10 minutes of browning, turn chicken's breast upwards and baste every 5 minutes. Serve with salad and chapatis or naan.

MARINATED FRIED CHICKEN

- *250 g (8 oz) boneless chicken—use thighs or breast*
- *1½ tablespoons Japanese soy sauce*
- *1 tablespoon sake or dry sherry*
- *1 teaspoon sugar*
- *2 tablespoons cornflour*
- *oil for deep frying*

Cut chicken into bite-size squares and marinate in a mixture of soy, sake and sugar for at least 1 hour. Drain chicken, roll pieces in cornflour and set aside for 10 minutes.

Heat oil in a deep frying pan to 170°C (350°F) and fry chicken in small batches for 2 to 3 minutes or until golden brown and crisp. Drain on paper towel and serve hot with rice.

An intensely flavoured but simple Thai dish. Don't be daunted, though, by the amount of garlic and black peppercorns! You can also cook the chicken on a barbecue.

GARLIC CHICKEN

- *500 g (1 lb) chicken thigh cutlets*
- *3 cloves garlic*
- *1 teaspoon salt, or to taste*
- *1 tablespoon black peppercorns*
- *2 whole plants fresh coriander, including roots*
- *1 tablespoon lemon juice*

Trim excess fat from chicken and slash flesh with a sharp knife twice or three times across each piece. Crush garlic with salt. Coarsely crush peppercorns with a mortar and pestle. Wash coriander and chop entire plants finely. Pound all together, mix with lemon juice and rub well into chicken pieces. Cover and marinate for at least 1 hour, or refrigerate overnight.

Preheat a griller until hot, or prepare a barbecue. Place chicken pieces about 15 cm (6 inches) from heat. Cook, turning every 5 minutes, until chicken is tender and skin crisp. Serve with white rice and salad.

CHICKEN OMELETTE

- *3 eggs*
- *2 tablespoons water*
- *salt to taste*
- *1 teaspoon Japanese soy sauce*
- *vegetable oil for frying*

FILLING
- *4 strips carrot and 4 green beans*
- *strips of cooked chicken breast*
- *2 teaspoons Japanese soy sauce*
- *1 teaspoon mirin or dry sherry*
- *1 teaspoon sugar*
- *1 teaspoon finely grated ginger*

FILLING Boil carrot strips and beans until just tender. Marinate chicken in remaining ingredients.

OMELETTE Beat eggs with fork. Add water, salt and soy sauce. Heat a large, heavy frying pan and oil lightly. Pour in half the egg and cook until set on bottom but still creamy on top. Place strips of chicken, carrot and beans at one end. Roll omelette firmly around Filling. Turn onto a warm plate. Repeat with rest of egg and Filling. Cut each omelette into slices and serve warm with steamed rice, or cold as an hors d'oeuvre.

Dried wood fungus (also known as 'cloud ears') swells to many times its size when reconstituted in water. It imparts no flavour of its own, but is prized in Chinese dishes for its resilient, crunchy texture.

BRAISED CHICKEN WITH WOOD FUNGUS

- 500 g (1 lb) chicken pieces
- 2 to 3 pieces wood fungus
- 1 small piece tender fresh ginger
- 1 small clove garlic
- pinch salt
- 5 pieces Szechwan pepper
- 1 tablespoon peanut oil
- 2 tablespoons dry sherry
- 2 teaspoons honey
- 1½ tablespoons light soy sauce
- 1 segment of star anise

Cut chicken with a sharp cleaver into bite-size pieces. Soak wood fungus in hot water for 10 minutes; drain and cut into small pieces. Scrape brown skin off ginger; cut into very thin slices and then into fine shreds until you have a tablespoonful. Crush garlic with pinch of salt. Lightly toast Szechwan pepper in a dry pan, then crush with a mortar and pestle or handle of a cleaver.

Heat a wok or heavy pan, add oil and fry ginger and

garlic over low heat just until pale golden. Add chicken pieces, increase heat to medium and stir-fry until chicken changes colour. Add crushed pepper, sherry, honey, soy sauce and star anise. Cover and simmer over low heat for 25 minutes, adding wood fungus pieces 5 minutes before end of cooking time. Add a little hot water if necessary.

CHICKEN AND BAMBOO SHOOT CURRY

- *500 g (1 lb) chicken pieces*
- *1 canned winter bamboo shoot*
- *1 medium onion, chopped finely*
- *2 tablespoons peanut oil*
- *1 tablespoon ground coriander*
- *½ teaspoon dried shrimp paste*
- *½ teaspoon galangal powder*
- *½ teaspoon chilli powder*
- *¾ cup canned coconut milk*
- *salt to taste*

Cut up any large pieces of chicken into smaller sections—for example, cleave thighs and breasts into halves. Drain bamboo shoots and cut into quarters, then into slices. Heat oil in a saucepan and fry onion over medium heat, stirring, until soft and golden. Add coriander, shrimp paste, galangal, chilli and salt. Fry, stirring constantly, for a few minutes until spices are browned.

Stir in chicken pieces until well mixed with spices. Add ¼ cup of the coconut milk mixed with ¾ cup water and bring to simmering point. Simmer over low heat for about 20 minutes. Stir in bamboo shoots and simmer for a further 20 minutes or until chicken is tender. Add remaining coconut milk and simmer, uncovered, stirring gently until heated through and oil rises to surface. Season to taste with salt. Serve this Indonesian dish with white rice, vegetables and accompaniments.

Chicken Livers with Chinese Broccoli

- 250 g (8 oz) chicken livers
- 2 slices fresh ginger
- 1 spring onion
- 2 tablespoons dark soy sauce
- 1 bunch Chinese broccoli (gai larn)
- 2 teaspoons sugar
- 1 tablespoon dry sherry
- 1 tablespoon peanut oil
- 1 teaspoon cornflour
- 1 teaspoon sesame oil
- 2 teaspoons white vinegar

Halve chicken livers and remove any tubes and connective tissue. Place in a small saucepan with ginger, spring onion cut into a few pieces, and 1 tablespoon of the soy sauce. Add sufficient boiling water just to cover livers. Simmer, covered, over low heat for 5 minutes. Drain, discarding ginger and onion.

Wash Chinese broccoli and slice diagonally. Combine remaining soy sauce with sugar and sherry. Heat peanut oil. Add chicken livers, tossing and stirring for 10 seconds. Add Chinese broccoli and stir-fry for 2 minutes. Pour in soy mixture, blend cornflour with 2 tablespoons of cold water and add, stirring until sauce thickens. Add sesame oil. Sprinkle vinegar around edge of wok and as it sizzles, quickly toss livers. Serve immediately.

CHICKEN AND MUSHROOMS WITH WALNUTS

- *4 dried shiitake (Chinese) mushrooms*
- *375 g (12 oz) chicken breast meat, skin removed*
- *2 teaspoons cornflour*
- *½ teaspoon salt, or to taste*
- *½ teaspoon five spice powder*
- *3 spring onions*
- *peanut oil for deep frying*
- *2 tablespoons peeled walnuts (see Note)*
- *¼ cup canned bamboo shoots, diced*
- *¼ cup chicken stock*
- *1 teaspoon light soy sauce*

Soak mushrooms in hot water for 30 minutes. Discard stems and slice caps across into strips. Cut chicken flesh into small dice. Mix half of cornflour with salt and five spice powder. Toss chicken pieces in this mixture. Cut spring onions into bite-size lengths. Heat oil in a wok and deep fry walnuts over medium heat for no more than 1 minute. Remove with a slotted spoon and drain on paper towel.

Fry chicken pieces in two batches in the same oil, just until they change colour—no longer than 1 minute. As they cook lift out with a slotted spoon and drain on paper towel. Pour off all but 1 tablespoon of oil.

Add mushrooms, spring onions and bamboo shoots to pan and stir-fry over high heat for 1 minute. Add chicken stock. Mix soy sauce with remaining cornflour and 1 tablespoon cold water. Stir into pan while bringing to boil. As sauce thickens add chicken pieces and heat through. Remove from heat, stir in walnuts and serve immediately.

Note   Peeled walnuts are sold in Chinese grocery stores. Alternatively blanch walnuts in boiling water for 1 minute, drain and cool. The thin skin should come away easily. The reason for removing this skin is that it is inclined to turn bitter if cooked on high heat.

DRY-FRIED CHICKEN

- 500 g (1 lb) chicken pieces—thighs, drumsticks or breast
- 1 tablespoon ghee or oil
- 1 large onion, thinly sliced
- ½ teaspoon chilli powder, or to taste
- ¼ cup plain yoghurt

MARINADE
- 1 small clove garlic, crushed
- ½ teaspoon grated fresh ginger
- ½ teaspoon garam masala
- ½ teaspoon salt, or to taste
- ½ teaspoon ground coriander
- ½ teaspoon ground cummin
- ¼ teaspoon ground turmeric
- 1 tablespoon plain yoghurt

Combine marinade ingredients and rub well over chicken pieces. Set aside for at least 1 hour.

Heat ghee or oil and fry onion, stirring constantly, until golden brown. Remove from pan with slotted spoon. In same pan fry chicken pieces until browned on both sides. Stir in chilli powder and any remaining marinade with ¼ cup water. Cover and simmer until tender. Return onions to pan; stir in yoghurt and serve with rice or naan.

In a stir-fried recipe like this one, preparation is just as important as the cooking. Having everything measured, ready and within reach is the secret behind this Chinese technique, surely one of the fastest cooking methods known.

Chicken in Black Bean Sauce

- *1 whole chicken breast*
- *3 stalks celery*
- *2 teaspoons canned salted black beans*
- *1 teaspoon soy sauce*
- *1 clove garlic, crushed*
- *½ teaspoon finely grated fresh ginger*
- *1 tablespoon dry sherry*
- *½ cup cold chicken stock*
- *1 teaspoon cornflour*
- *1 tablespoon oil*

Cut chicken meat from bone and dice. Cut celery in thin diagonal slices. Rinse black beans and mash with a fork. Add soy sauce, garlic, ginger, sherry and half of chicken stock; mix well. Stir cornflour into remaining chicken stock.

Heat oil in a wok; add chicken and stir-fry, tossing for 2 minutes. Pour in black bean mixture and stir until boiling. Add cornflour mixture, stirring constantly, until it boils and thickens—about 1 minute. Add celery slices and toss in sauce for 1 minute more. Serve immediately with steamed rice.

MEAT DISHES

In India, and even in parts of the UK where there are sizable Indian populations, fresh fenugreek herb is easily obtained. But until this herb becomes more popular in other countries, we must use spinach and flavour the dish with dried fenugreek leaves.

INDIAN LAMB WITH FENUGREEK

- ½ bunch spinach leaves
- 250 g (8 oz) boneless lamb
- 1 tablespoon ghee or mustard oil
- 1 onion, finely chopped
- 1 small clove garlic, finely chopped
- 1 teaspoon finely chopped fresh ginger
- ½ teaspoon chilli powder
- ½ teaspoon ground turmeric
- 1 ripe tomato, peeled and chopped
- 1 teaspoon salt, or to taste
- little hot water
- 1 tablespoon dried fenugreek leaves
- ½ teaspoon garam masala
- ½ teaspoon kalonji (nigella) seeds

Wash spinach leaves, discarding any tough stalks. Cut lamb into bite-size cubes. Heat ghee or oil and fry onion, garlic and ginger over low heat, stirring frequently, until soft and golden. Stir in chilli powder and turmeric; add lamb and fry, stirring, until colour changes. Add tomato and salt with a little hot water. Cover and simmer over very low heat until meat is almost tender. Add a little more hot water if liquid evaporates. Add spinach, dried fenugreek, garam masala and kalonji seeds; continue cooking until spinach is cooked to a pulp and meat is tender. Serve hot with rice and accompaniments.

MINCED MEAT AND POTATO CURRY

- *1 tablespoon oil or ghee*
- *1 medium onion, finely chopped*
- *1 small clove garlic, finely chopped*
- *½ teaspoon finely grated fresh ginger*
- *½ teaspoon ground turmeric*
- *1 teaspoon ground coriander*
- *½ teaspoon ground cummin*
- *¼ teaspoon chilli powder*
- *1 teaspoon salt, or to taste*
- *1 tablespoon lemon juice*
- *250 g (8 oz) minced lamb or beef*
- *250 g (8 oz) potatoes, peeled and quartered*
- *½ teaspoon garam masala*
- *1 tablespoon chopped fresh mint*

Heat oil or ghee in a heavy saucepan and fry onions, garlic and ginger, stirring frequently, until soft and golden. Stir in turmeric, coriander, cummin and chilli powder, frying for 1 minute. Add salt and lemon juice, and when mixture starts to sizzle, add meat and cook until browned, stirring constantly to break up any lumps.

Add potatoes and ½ cup hot water and bring to a simmer. Cover and cook over low heat for about 30 minutes or until potatoes and meat are tender. Stir occasionally towards the end of cooking time to prevent curry from sticking to base of pan. Sprinkle with garam masala; stir gently. Garnish with chopped mint. Serve with Indian bread or rice, and a sambal or other accompaniment.

Lamb and Apricot Curry

- *90 g (3 oz) dried apricot halves*
- *375 g (12 oz) boneless lean lamb*
- *3 dried red chillies, seeds removed*
- *2 teaspoons chopped fresh ginger*
- *2 teaspoons chopped fresh garlic*
- *1 teaspoon ground cummin*
- *1 tablespoon ghee or oil*
- *1 medium onion, finely chopped*
- *½ teaspoon ground cinnamon*
- *¼ teaspoon ground cloves*
- *¼ teaspoon ground black pepper*
- *¼ teaspoon ground cardamom*
- *1 large ripe tomato, peeled, seeded and chopped*
- *1 teaspoon salt, or to taste*
- *1 teaspoon brown sugar*
- *2 teaspoons malt vinegar*
- *1 tablespoon chopped fresh coriander leaves*

Soak apricots in water for 30 minutes, then drain. Cut meat into bite-size pieces. Soak chillies in hot water for 10 minutes. Put ginger, garlic, cummin and chillies into a blender container and grind to a paste, adding a little water if necessary. Mix half of paste with meat and marinate for 1 hour.

Heat ghee or oil in a heavy saucepan or flameproof casserole and fry onion until golden brown. Add remaining paste with cinnamon, cloves, pepper and cardamom. Stir well, then add meat and fry until browned. Add tomato and salt; cover and cook on low heat until lamb is tender, adding a little hot water if necessary. Add brown sugar, vinegar and apricots and simmer over very low heat for 15 minutes. Garnish with chopped coriander and serve with rice or chapati and a choice of accompaniments.

Stir-fried Pork with Bean Sprouts

- *250 g (8 oz) pork fillet or other lean cut*
- *1 clove garlic*
- *½ teaspoon salt, or to taste*
- *½ teaspoon grated fresh ginger*
- *½ teaspoon five spice powder*
- *1 punnet bean sprouts*
- *1 teaspoon cornflour*
- *1 tablespoon soy sauce*
- *1 tablespoon peanut oil*
- *2 teaspoons sesame oil*

Remove any fat from pork and cut into very thin slices, then cut these slices into fine shreds. Crush garlic with salt and rub garlic, ginger and five spice powder thoroughly into pork. Wash bean sprouts; drain well. Mix cornflour and soy sauce with 2 tablespoons water.

Heat peanut and sesame oils in a wok; add pork when hot and stir-fry over high heat, tossing constantly, for 2 minutes or until meat changes colour. Add bean sprouts and stir-fry for 1 minute. Add cornflour mixture and stir until it boils and thickens slightly. Toss until pork and bean sprouts are coated with sauce. Serve immediately.

GARLIC BEEF AND MUSTARD CABBAGE

- *250 g (8 oz) fillet or rump steak*
- *4 dried shiitake (Chinese) mushrooms*
- *125 g (4 oz) mustard cabbage (gai choy)*
- *2 tablespoons dark soy sauce*
- *1 tablespoon sugar*
- *2 cloves garlic*
- *salt to taste*
- *2 tablespoons peanut oil*
- *1 teaspoon sesame oil*

SAUCE

- *2 teaspoons dry sherry*
- *2 teaspoons dark soy sauce*
- *1 tablespoon oyster sauce*
- *½ teaspoon sugar*
- *1 teaspoon cornflour*

Remove any fat from steak and slice meat thinly across the grain. Soak mushrooms in hot water for 30 minutes. Discard stems, cut caps in halves and simmer 15 minutes in soaking water with soy sauce and sugar. Drain. Wash cabbage well and drain. Discard any tough ends of outer leaves and slice cabbage diagonally. Crush garlic with a little salt. Combine Sauce ingredients in a small bowl.

Heat a wok; add 1 tablespoon of the peanut oil and swirl to coat. Add beef and stir-fry over high heat, tossing until colour changes. Remove to a plate. Add remaining peanut oil to wok. When hot add cabbage, garlic and mushrooms and stir-fry for 1 minute. Return meat to wok and continue to cook for 30 seconds. Add Sauce mixture and stir through. Remove from heat and stir in sesame oil. Serve immediately with rice.

MONGOLIAN LAMB

- *250 g (8 oz) lamb fillets or lamb leg chops*
- *½ teaspoon sugar*
- *½ teaspoon salt, or to taste*
- *1 tablespoon dark soy sauce*
- *1 small egg*
- *2 teaspoons cornflour*
- *2 tablespoons peanut oil*
- *1 teaspoon finely chopped garlic*
- *1 onion, cut in eighths*
- *2 teaspoons ground bean sauce*
- *¼ teaspoon five spice powder*
- *1 teaspoon hoi sin sauce*
- *1 teaspoon chilli bean sauce*
- *2 teaspoons dry sherry*

Trim any fat from meat and remove bones as necessary. Cut into bite-size, paper-thin slices. (This is easier if you partially freeze meat first.) Soak in cold water for 30 minutes. Rinse until water runs clear; then drain and squeeze out excess water.

In a bowl mix sugar, salt, soy sauce, egg, and cornflour. Add lamb to bowl and mix well. Stir in 2 teaspoons of peanut oil. Leave to marinate for 30 minutes.

Heat a wok; add 1 tablespoon of oil. Stir-fry lamb over very high heat until colour changes. Remove lamb with slotted spoon. Add remaining oil and stir-fry garlic and onion over medium heat 1 minute. Add ground bean sauce, five spice powder, hoi sin sauce and chilli bean sauce. Return lamb and toss over high heat. Add sherry and serve.

The beef for this dish is tenderised with bicarbonate of soda. However, you can use more tender cuts and omit this step.

SHREDDED BEEF WITH ASPARAGUS

- 250 g (8 oz) round or other lean steak
- ¼ teaspoon bicarbonate of soda
- 1 onion
- ½ bunch asparagus
- 2 tablespoons peanut oil

MARINADE

- 1 teaspoon dark soy sauce
- 1 teaspoon cornflour
- ½ teaspoon sugar
- 2 teaspoons dry sherry

SAUCE

- 2 teaspoons light soy sauce
- 2 teaspoons oyster sauce
- 1 teaspoon cornflour

Remove any fat from steak and cut into fine shreds. Dissolve bicarbonate of soda in 2 tablespoons of water. Add to meat, kneading well until all liquid is absorbed. Refrigerate for at least 2 hours.

Cut onion in half lengthwise, then cut each half lengthwise

into four wedges. Snap any tough ends off asparagus and discard. Cut stalks diagonally into 5 cm (2 inch) lengths.

Combine Marinade ingredients and mix well into meat. Leave to marinate for about 20 minutes. Mix Sauce ingredients with 1 tablespoon water. Heat a wok, add 1 tablespoon of peanut oil and stir-fry onions over high heat for 1 minute. With a slotted spoon transfer onions to a plate. Add asparagus to wok and stir-fry, tossing for 1 minute. Remove asparagus to a plate. Add remaining tablespoon of oil to wok and when hot add meat and stir-fry, tossing over high heat until its colour changes. Put meat aside with onions.

Wipe out wok and return asparagus. Add 2 tablespoons hot water. Cover wok and cook for 3 minutes or until asparagus is tender but still crisp. Add Sauce mixture and stir until it boils and thickens slightly. Return beef and onions to wok and toss together until heated through. Serve at once with rice.

A Tenderising Trick

When time is short and you need tender meat, buy fillet or rump for your stir-fried dishes. But when there's time to plan ahead you can make considerable savings by buying lean, round blade or skirt steak and using the following technique. Place the meat in the freezer to make it firm enough to cut into paper-thin slices. Dissolve ½ teaspoon of bicarbonate of soda in 3 tablespoons of water and pour over meat. This is sufficient for 500 g (1 lb) of meat. Knead until liquid is absorbed. Refrigerate for at least 2 hours, or overnight. Cook as directed and it will be as tender as fillet steak.

Use this marinade on squid also, which is inclined to be tough.

It is not always necessary to use expensive cuts of beef when stir-frying. You can tenderise a cheaper cut by marinating it with bicarbonate of soda, and since the vegetables are cooked separately there is little loss of vitamins.

CHILLI BEEF WITH CELERY

- 250 g (8 oz) round or skirt steak
- ¼ teaspoon bicarbonate of soda
- 2 stalks celery
- 2 teaspoons canned salted black beans
- 2 teaspoons dark soy sauce
- 1 teaspoon chilli bean sauce
- ½ teaspoon sugar
- 1 teaspoon cornflour
- 2 tablespoons peanut oil
- 1 teaspoon crushed garlic

Remove any fat from meat and slice steak thinly across the grain. Dissolve bicarbonate of soda in 2 tablespoons of hot water. Knead well into meat until all liquid is absorbed. Cover and refrigerate for at least 2 hours.

Wash celery and cut across into 1.5 cm (½ inch) slices. Rinse black beans under cold water, drain and chop. Mix together soy sauce, chilli bean sauce, sugar and cornflour with 2 tablespoons cold water.

Heat a wok and add 1 tablespoon of the oil, swirling to coat inside. When hot stir-fry beef over high heat, tossing until browned. Remove to a plate. Add remaining oil and stir-fry celery for 2 minutes. Remove with slotted spoon. Add garlic to oil remaining in pan and stir-fry for a few seconds. Add black beans and stir-fry for a few seconds more. Stir in sauce mixture, cooking until it boils and thickens. Return celery to wok and simmer for 2 minutes. Add beef and stir until reheated through. Serve immediately with hot steamed rice.

Delicious for a barbecue. Since the meat has been cooked before being moulded, it requires only a short cooking time to brown the outer surface.

Minced Lamb and Lentil Patties

- *375 g (12 oz) finely minced lamb*
- *1 small onion, finely chopped*
- *1½ tablespoons red lentils*
- *1 teaspoon finely grated fresh ginger*
- *½ teaspoon finely chopped garlic*
- *salt to taste*
- *½ teaspoon garam masala*
- *1 tablespoon plain yoghurt*
- *ghee or oil for shallow frying*

Filling
- *1 small fresh green chilli, seeded and finely chopped*
- *2 teaspoons finely chopped fresh coriander*
- *1 small spring onion, finely chopped*

Place lamb with onion, lentils, ginger, garlic, salt and 1 cup water into a heavy-based saucepan and bring to boil, stirring frequently. Cover and cook over low heat until meat, lentils and onion are soft—about 45 minutes. Uncover and cook, stirring occasionally, until all liquid is absorbed. This may take 1 hour. Set aside to cool. Add garam masala and yoghurt; mix well. Knead until mixture is completely smooth.

Combine Filling ingredients. Divide lamb mixture into 4 portions, forming each into a flat circle. Put a quarter of Filling in the centre of each circle and close mixture around it, pinching edges together. Flatten gently to form a small round patty. Shallow fry in a heavy pan lightly greased with ghee or oil, or on a heavy griddle over a barbecue. Serve hot.

This curry has a very dark colour because in Sri Lanka (or Ceylon as it used to be called) the spices are traditionally roasted. Ceylon curry powder, which is a really dark coffee brown, will give the dish the correct flavour. There is probably enough for 3 or 4 servings but it keeps well in the refrigerator, or can be frozen.

Sri Lankan Pork Curry

- 500 g (1 lb) boneless pork shoulder, loin or belly
- 1 tablespoon oil
- 4 curry leaves
- 1 small onion, finely chopped
- 1 large clove garlic, finely chopped
- ½ teaspoon finely grated fresh ginger
- 1 teaspoon tamarind pulp, dissolved in ½ cup hot water
- 1 tablespoon Ceylon curry powder
- ½ teaspoon chilli powder
- salt to taste
- 1 teaspoon vinegar
- small piece cinnamon stick
- 2 cardamom pods
- ⅓ cup canned coconut milk

Remove excess fat from pork and cut into large cubes. Heat oil in a heavy saucepan and fry curry leaves until they start to brown. Add onion, garlic and ginger and fry, stirring frequently over low heat until onion is soft and golden.

Add curry powder, chilli powder, salt, vinegar and pork to saucepan. Stir-fry over high heat until meat is thoroughly coated with spice mixture. Add tamarind liquid, cinnamon and cardamom and cook, covered, over low heat until pork is tender—about 1 hour. Add coconut milk and simmer for about 10 minutes, uncovered, or until sauce is thick and dark. Serve with plain steamed rice, Bitter Melon Sambol (see p. 76) and Coconut Sambol (see p. 80).

The sweet, mild flavour of pumpkin offsets the heat which may be inherent in the curry.

BEEF AND PUMPKIN CURRY

- *250 g (8 oz) stewing steak*
- *250 g (8 oz) pumpkin*
- *1 tablespoon peanut oil*
- *1 tablespoon Thai Red Curry Paste (see p. 11)*
- *½ cup canned coconut milk*
- *2 kaffir lime leaves*
- *1 large dried red chilli*
- *2 teaspoons fish sauce*
- *½ teaspoon palm sugar or brown sugar*

Trim any fat from beef and cut into cubes. Peel pumpkin, discarding seeds, and cut into cubes of same size. Heat oil in a heavy saucepan or wok and fry Red Curry Paste, stirring, over medium heat until it smells fragrant and oil appears around the edges. Add beef and stir-fry until colour changes.

Add half of coconut milk with ½ cup water and lime leaves, chilli and fish sauce. Simmer for 30 minutes. Add pumpkin and stir well. (If necessary add extra water so that there is sufficient liquid to simmer pumpkin.) Simmer for a further 35 minutes or until pumpkin and beef are tender. Stir in sugar until it dissolves and then remaining coconut milk until heated through. Serve with rice.

RICE, NOODLES, BREADS

This is an important section because, not only are rice, noodles and bread (not your supermarket sliced white!) the basis of every Asian meal, but you will find great variety, even within the country whose cooking you are sampling.

RICE

In Asia rice is cooked with or without salt. For example, India, Sri Lanka and other curry-eating countries usually add salt, whereas Thailand, Vietnam, China and Japan cook rice without salt because most dishes are flavoured with salty soy sauce or fish sauce.

Short or medium grain rice is the correct type to use for Japanese and Chinese meals as it clings together and is easily handled with chopsticks. Long grain rice, however, has become common in Chinese restaurants here because westerners prefer it.

Basmati rice, with its strong, very individual fragrance, is ideal with Indian meals and particularly lends itself to pilau and biriani.

For Thai meals it is customary to serve jasmine rice, a long grain variety with a faint perfume, which cooks easily and has neither the graininess of basmati nor the clinging texture of short or medium grain.

NOODLES

If you cannot buy a particular kind of noodle and decide to substitute it with another, make sure you check the cooking time. For example, bean starch noodles require 15 to 20 minutes boiling, whereas wheat noodles of a similar thickness require only 2 minutes.

One important thing never stated on noodle packets (I refer in particular to the bundles of egg noodles) is that if dropped into boiling water the inner parts will stick together and be inedible. The solution is not difficult: you just soak the bundles in a bowl of warm water. In about 10 minutes the strands will separate beautifully. Drain the noodles and drop them into boiling water for the required cooking time: thin noodles are done in a couple of minutes; thick take a minute or two longer.

Rice noodles are different again. Fine rice vermicelli, or rice sticks as some brands label them, require soaking in hot water for 10 minutes, or 2 minutes in boiling water. The thicker rice noodles must be boiled and require longer cooking time.

Certainly use fresh rice and wheat noodles if you can get them, but I have concentrated here on readily available dried noodles.

Bean thread vermicelli is something I recommend buying in small bundles. If you buy a large bundle and need only a little, you will have a hard time separating it from the mother skein. I have seldom tangled with anything so obstinate. Try pulling it away and it seems to have no end; try cutting it with scissors and it is so tough you get sore red marks on thumb and forefinger. Packs already divided into 50 g bundles are most convenient to use.

BREADS

There are many breads in Asian cuisines, but you need only three Indian varieties to accompany the dishes in this book—chapatis, puris and naan. Chapatis are the daily bread of most Indians and are very thin discs cooked on a griddle. Amazingly they are quite light. Puris are similar but deep fried, so are somewhat richer. Naan is yeast-risen and baked. Even without the traditional earthen oven these breads are quite delicious.

An Indian rice dish suitable for serving with meat or vegetable curries.

SPICY RICE

- 1 cup long grain or basmati rice
- 1 tablespoon ghee
- 1 tablespoon oil
- 1 large onion, finely sliced
- 1 cardamom pod, bruised
- 1 small piece cinnamon stick
- 2 whole cloves
- 6 whole black peppercorns
- ¼ teaspoon ground turmeric
- 1 teaspoon salt
- 2 tablespoons raw cashew nuts, split in halves
- 6 fresh or dried curry leaves
- 1 fresh green chilli, seeded and sliced
- ¾ teaspoon black mustard seeds
- 1 tablespoon chopped fresh coriander
- 2 tablespoons grated fresh coconut, or desiccated coconut

Wash rice well and set aside to drain in a sieve for 30 minutes. Heat half of ghee and oil in a heavy saucepan and fry onion with whole spices until onion is golden; stir frequently. Add turmeric and rice to pan and fry, stirring carefully with a slotted metal spoon, until grains are coated with ghee. Add 2 cups hot water with salt; stir well and bring to boil. Cover with a tight-fitting lid and turn heat very low. Cook for 20 to 25 minutes without lifting lid.

Heat remaining ghee and oil in a small pan and fry cashew nuts until golden; remove with slotted spoon. Fry curry leaves, green chillies and mustard seeds until seeds pop. Uncover pan and pour fried mixture over rice, lightly forking it through. Turn rice onto serving plate and garnish with fried cashews, chopped coriander leaves and grated coconut.

Short or medium grain rice cooked by this absorption method is the staple food of China and Japan. Although mainly served as the basis for a meal, accompanied by other dishes, it can also be mixed with a variety of ingredients.

STEAMED RICE

- *1 cup short or medium grain rice*
- *1½ cups cold water*

Wash rice several times in cold water. Leave to drain in a sieve for at least 30 minutes. Put rice in a heavy-based saucepan, add cold water and bring rapidly to boil. Cover pan with a tight-fitting lid, turn heat low and cook for 15 minutes without lifting lid. Turn heat high for 20 seconds and, still without uncovering, remove pan from heat and leave to stand for 10 minutes before serving. If making fried rice, turn onto a tray immediately and leave until completely cold.

Note   For long grain rice, increase water to 2 cups.

RICE WITH CHICKEN AND MUSHROOMS

- *1 quantity of short grain rice (see p. 50)*
- *4 dried shiitake (Chinese) mushrooms*
- *2 tablespoons Japanese soy sauce*
- *2 tablespoons mirin or dry sherry*
- *1 tablespoon sugar*
- *185 g (6 oz) boned chicken breast, thinly sliced*
- *1 egg, beaten*
- *salt to taste*
- *½ cup cooked green peas*

Soak dried mushrooms in very hot water for 30 minutes. Remove and discard stems; reserve soaking water. Put caps in a small saucepan with ¼ cup of soaking water and half each of the soy, mirin and sugar. Bring to boil, cover and cook until liquid is almost evaporated. Remove mushrooms from pan and allow to cool.

Put remaining soy, mirin and sugar with 2 tablespoons soaking water into the same saucepan. Add chicken and bring to boil; turn heat low, cover and simmer gently for 3 minutes. Remove from heat and leave covered.

Cook rice following recipe for Steamed Rice. Meanwhile beat egg lightly with salt and cook in a lightly greased frying pan to make 1 large, thin, flat omelette. Take care that it does not brown. Turn onto a flat plate and when cool cut into narrow strips.

When rice is cooked spoon it into a large earthenware bowl with lid. Spread chicken on surface of rice; spoon liquid over. Slice mushrooms and spread on top of chicken. Decorate with omelette strips and green peas. Serve hot.

YELLOW RICE

- *1 cup long grain rice*
- *1 tablespoon ghee*
- *1 small onion, finely sliced*
- *2 cloves*
- *6 black peppercorns*
- *4 cardamom pods, bruised*
- *½ teaspoon ground turmeric*
- *1 teaspoon salt*
- *4 dried curry leaves*
- *small piece lemon grass, lightly crushed*
- *1 cup canned coconut milk*

Wash rice and leave to drain thoroughly in a sieve. Heat ghee in a heavy saucepan, add onion and fry until it starts to turn golden. Stir in cloves, peppercorns, cardamom pods, turmeric, salt, curry leaves and lemon grass. Add rice and fry, stirring constantly, for 2 to 3 minutes until rice is well coated with ghee and turmeric. Mix coconut milk with 1 cup water; add to pan, stir to mix, and bring to boil. Reduce heat to very low. Cover pan tightly and cook for 20 minutes.

When rice is cooked, fluff up lightly with a fork, removing whole spices. Serve hot with curries and accompaniments.

Thai Fried Rice

- *2 cups cold steamed rice*
- *1½ tablespoons peanut oil*
- *1 medium onion, finely chopped*
- *125 g (4 oz) raw prawns, shelled and deveined*
- *185 g (6 oz) can crab meat, drained*
- *1 large egg, beaten*
- *1 tablespoon fish sauce*
- *1 teaspoon chilli sauce*
- *1 tablespoon tomato paste*
- *½ cup chopped spring onions*
- *1 tablespoon chopped fresh coriander leaves*

Heat oil in a wok or heavy frying pan and fry onion on medium low heat, stirring occasionally, until soft and translucent. Increase heat to high. Add prawns and crab meat and fry for 3 minutes. Push to side of wok or pan. Pour beaten egg into centre of wok and stir until just beginning to set. Add rice, toss and stir until rice is heated through. Combine fish sauce, chilli sauce and tomato paste, pour over rice and toss thoroughly so that rice has a reddish colour. Remove from heat and stir in spring onions. Transfer to warm serving platter, garnish with chopped coriander leaves and serve.

Prawn Fried Rice in Omelette

- 1 tablespoon oil
- 2 spring onions, chopped
- 1 fresh chilli, seeded and sliced
- 2 teaspoons Thai Red Curry Paste (see p. 11)
- 125 g (4 oz) uncooked medium-size prawns,
  shelled and deveined
- 1½ cups cold cooked rice
- 2 teaspoons fish sauce
- 2 teaspoons lime or lemon juice
- 1 small clove garlic, crushed

Omelette and Garnish
- 4 eggs
- pinch salt
- oil
- spring onion leaves

Heat a wok and add oil. On medium heat fry spring onions and chillies, stirring, until softened. Add Red Curry Paste and cook, stirring, until fragrant. Add prawns and stir-fry until they change colour. Stir in rice, tossing until heated through. Remove from heat. Combine fish sauce, lime juice and garlic and sprinkle over rice, toss to distribute flavours. Transfer rice mixture to a bowl, cover and keep warm.

Omelette Beat eggs with salt and 1 tablespoon cold water. Heat a large, well-seasoned frying pan, add 2 teaspoons of oil and swirl to coat surface. Pour in half of beaten egg mixture and swirl to make large, thin sheet of egg. Cook over low heat until almost set.

Place half of rice mixture in centre. Fold all four edges over, like an envelope, to enclose rice. Press down well, then slip a wide metal spatula underneath and gently turn over. Lift onto a plate. Repeat with remaining mixtures.

Garnish Use spring onion leaves blanched in boiling water just until limp, to tie each omelette parcel. Serve with a small dish of commercial chilli sauce.

Chicken thigh fillets are the best type of meat for this recipe as they stay nicely moist. Breast fillets may be used, but take care to cook them very briefly or they will be dry.

CHILLI CHICKEN WITH NOODLES

- *125 g (4 oz) boneless chicken*
- *2 tablespoons peanut oil*
- *1 dried red chilli*
- *2 teaspoons dried garlic flakes*
- *¼ cup peanuts*
- *1 tablespoon Thai Red Curry Paste (see p. 11)*
- *1 tablespoon fish sauce*
- *125 g (4 oz) fine rice vermicelli, soaked and drained (see Note)*
- *1 tablespoon lime juice*
- *¼ cup sliced spring onions*
- *¼ cup chopped fresh coriander leaves*

Remove skin and any fat from chicken and cut meat into strips. Heat oil and fry dried chilli over medium heat until blackened and puffed. Drain on paper towel. In the same oil fry garlic flakes on low heat for a few seconds, lifting out with a wire strainer as soon as they turn pale golden. Drain. Add peanuts and fry, stirring constantly, until light brown. Lift out and drain on paper towel. Remove stalk from chilli, shake out seeds and crumble chilli into small pieces. Crush garlic flakes and peanuts. Mix all three together and set aside.

Add Red Curry Paste to wok and stir-fry for 2 minutes. Add chicken strips and toss over medium-high heat until colour changes. Add 2 tablespoons water and fish sauce. Boil for 1 minute, then add noodles, lime juice and spring onions. Toss thoroughly in spicy mixture until heated through. Serve sprinkled with peanut mixture and coriander leaves.

Note Fine rice vermicelli only needs to be soaked for 10 minutes in hot water before draining and adding to this recipe.

Served cold or at room temperature, this is ideal for a light summer luncheon or to take on a picnic.

NOODLE SALAD

- 125 g (4 oz) egg noodles
- 2 spring onions
- 1 egg, beaten
- pinch salt
- peanut oil for frying
- 125 g (4 oz) fresh bean sprouts
- 125 g (4 oz) fresh, firm bean curd
- 1 tablespoon peanut oil
- ½ teaspoon crushed garlic
- 1 tablespoon sesame oil
- 1 tablespoon light soy sauce
- 2 tablespoons chopped fresh coriander leaves

Cook noodles in plenty of lightly salted boiling water just until tender—test regularly to make sure they don't overcook. If they are in tight little bundles, soak them in warm water first for the strands to loosen so they cook evenly. When cooked, add cold water to the pan, then drain noodles in a colander and sprinkle with a teaspoonful of oil.

Finely chop one spring onion. Combine beaten egg with salt and chopped spring onion. Heat a heavy frying pan and lightly grease base with paper towel dipped in peanut oil. Pour in beaten egg mixture, tilting pan so that mixture spreads to form a thin omelette. Cook over low heat just until set, without browning, then turn out onto a plate. Leave to cool. Wash and drain bean sprouts. Cut bean curd into thin strips.

Heat a wok; add 1 tablespoon peanut oil and fry garlic for a few seconds—do not let it brown. Add bean sprouts and toss for 30 seconds. Remove from heat and allow to cool.

In a serving bowl, toss together noodles, garlic, bean sprouts and bean curd. Mix sesame oil and soy sauce to make a dressing; pour over noodles; toss. Roll up omelette and cut across into narrow slices. Add omelette strips to bowl; cover and refrigerate.

Slice remaining spring onion into diagonal pieces and use with coriander leaves to garnish salad when serving.

TRANSPARENT NOODLES WITH PORK

- 50 g (1½ oz) bean thread vermicelli
- 3 dried shiitake (Chinese) mushrooms
- 90 g (3 oz) boneless pork
- 2 teaspoons dry sherry
- 2 teaspoons light soy sauce
- salt to taste
- ⅓ cup chicken stock
- 1 teaspoon cornflour
- 1 tablespoon peanut oil
- 2 spring onions, finely chopped
- 1 teaspoon finely grated fresh ginger
- 1 tablespoon chilli bean sauce
- 1 small red capsicum, seeded and finely chopped
- 2 tablespoons chopped fresh coriander leaves

Place noodles in a large bowl and cover with boiling water. Set aside for 20 minutes or until noodles are soft and transparent. Drain and cut into short lengths with a sharp knife. Soak mushrooms in hot water for 30 minutes; squeeze dry, discard stems and dice caps finely.

Cut pork into small dice. Mix sherry, soy sauce, salt, stock and cornflour in a small bowl. Heat a wok over high heat; add peanut oil and swirl to coat surface. When oil is hot add pork and mushrooms and stir-fry until cooked and browned. Add spring onions and ginger, stir for a few seconds, then add chilli bean sauce and chopped capsicum. Cook over medium heat for 1 minute—mixture should be aromatic and look cooked.

Stir in sherry mixture until it boils. Add noodles and simmer, stirring, until liquid has reduced. Stir in coriander leaves and serve at once, garnished with a coriander sprig.

CHILLED BUCKWHEAT NOODLES

- *100 g (3½ oz) soba (buckwheat noodles)*
- *1 sheet toasted nori (dried laver seaweed)*
- *100 g (3½ oz) frozen fish cakes, sliced*
- *2 teaspoons finely grated fresh ginger*
- *3 spring onions, very finely sliced*
- *1 cup dashi*
- *¼ cup Japanese soy sauce*
- *¼ cup mirin or dry sherry*
- *salt or sugar to taste*

Drop noodles into a large pot of boiling water. When water returns to boil add 1 cup cold water. Bring to boil again and cook just until noodles are tender enough to bite—about 2 minutes. Drain in a colander and keep running cold water through noodles until quite cold. Drain well.

Cut a piece of nori in fine shreds with scissors. Put noodles and fish cakes on plates and sprinkle nori over.

Heat remaining ingredients in a small pan. Cool. Pour into individual sauce dishes. Put small portions of ginger and spring onion on each plate. Stir into sauce and dip noodles before eating.

Rice Vermicelli with Beef and Long Beans

- *185 g (6 oz) lean steak*
- *125 g (4 oz) rice vermicelli*
- *185 g (6 oz) long (snake) beans*
- *1 tablespoon peanut oil*
- *1 small clove garlic, crushed*
- *½ teaspoon finely grated fresh ginger*
- *½ cup beef stock*
- *salt to taste*
- *1 tablespoon light soy sauce*
- *chilli oil, optional*

Partially freeze steak until firm—this helps when slicing. Soak rice vermicelli in a large bowl of cold water for 10 minutes, then drain well. Slice beef very thinly. Trim beans and cut into 5 cm (2 inch) lengths. Heat oil in a wok and stir-fry beans for 2 minutes. Remove and set aside. Add garlic, ginger and beef, tossing until beef changes colour; then add stock, salt and soy sauce. Add rice vermicelli and toss until heated through. Cover and cook on fairly low heat for 3 minutes. Return beans to wok and toss with other ingredients for 1 minute. Serve immediately, offering chilli oil separately for sprinkling on individual servings to taste.

CHAPATIS (UNLEAVENED INDIAN BREAD)
Makes 6 x 18 cm (7 inch) discs

- 1 cup fine wholemeal flour or roti flour
- salt to taste
- 1 teaspoon ghee or oil
- ⅓ cup lukewarm water

Put flour into a mixing bowl. Mix in salt and then rub in ghee or oil. Add water all at once and mix into a firm but not stiff dough. Knead for at least 10 minutes. Form dough into a ball, cover with plastic wrap and set aside for at least 1 hour. (If left overnight the dough will make very light chapatis.)

Shape dough into balls about the size of a walnut. Roll each one to a 18 cm (7 inch) circle on a lightly floured board. Once all chapatis are rolled, heat a heavy ungreased frying pan or griddle plate until very hot. Cook chapatis on low heat, starting with those that were rolled out first since a brief resting time helps them to puff. Cook chapati for 1 minute, then turn over and cook other side for another minute or so, pressing lightly around the edge with a folded tea towel. This encourages bubbles to form and makes the chapati lighter. As each one is cooked wrap in a clean towel until all are ready. Serve immediately with dry curries or vegetable dishes.

PURIS (DEEP-FRIED INDIAN BREAD)

Proceed as for chapatis. After 1 hour in plastic wrap, divide into 16 equal portions and roll out to perfect circles, 10 cm (4 inches) across. Heat about 2.5 cm (1 inch) oil in a wok or deep frying pan. When a light haze rises from the oil, fry puris one at a time over medium heat. Spoon hot oil over puri as it cooks until it puffs up. Turn with a spatula and fry other side. When both sides are pale golden brown, drain on absorbent paper. Makes 16 x 10 cm (4 inch) puris.

Naan (leavened Indian bread)

- 15 g (½ oz) fresh compressed yeast
or 1½ teaspoons active dried yeast
  - ⅓ cup warm water
  - 1 teaspoon sugar
  - ¼ cup plain yoghurt
    - 1 small egg
  - 60 g (2 oz) butter, melted
    - 1 teaspoon salt
  - 2½ cups plain (all-purpose) flour
- 1 tablespoon kalonji (nigella) seeds or sesame seeds

Dissolve yeast in warm water, add sugar and set aside in a warm place until yeast froths. If it does not bubble in 10 minutes, start again with fresh yeast.

Beat together yoghurt, egg, butter, salt and yeast mixture. Add half of flour; beat briskly until smooth, then add remaining flour by hand to form a firm dough. Knead for 10 minutes or until dough is smooth and elastic, dusting hands lightly with flour when necessary. Put dough into a warm, greased bowl, cover and leave in a warm place until double in bulk. Punch down and divide into 4 equal portions.

Shape each portion of dough into flat, pear-shaped loaves. They should be thin in the centre and have a thicker rim. Smooth some of the extra yoghurt over each one with the back of a spoon and sprinkle with kalonji or sesame seeds. Leave to rise 15 minutes. Preheat oven to very hot—230°C (450°F)—and put two ungreased baking trays into oven to preheat. Remove baking trays from oven using oven mitts. Place two loaves on each tray and return to oven; bake for 10 to 12 minutes or until puffed and golden.

Serve warm or at room temperature with dry preparations such as Curried Dried Beans (see p. 63) or Tandoori Chicken (see p. 25).

Note Any leftover naan can be wrapped and frozen to be reheated when required.

VEGETABLES AND SALADS

Some of these recipes are substantial dishes which can be served as main course when accompanied by rice or bread. Others are used more as side dishes, but are nonetheless important because they provide nutritional value and a variety of flavours and textures typical of Asian-style meals.

STIR-FRIED GREEN VEGETABLES

- 1 tablespoon peanut oil
- 1 clove garlic, crushed
- ½ teaspoon finely grated fresh ginger
- 1 cup green beans, sliced diagonally
- 1 cup broccoli florets
- 1 cup Brussels sprouts, quartered lengthwise
- salt to taste
- ½ cup chicken stock
- 2 teaspoons sesame oil

Heat a wok, add oil and swirl to coat. Add garlic and ginger; stir-fry for a few seconds. Add vegetables and toss over high heat until they turn a brilliant green. Add salt and stock. Cover and steam for 2 minutes. Vegetables should be tender but still crisp. Sprinkle sesame oil over and serve immediately with rice.

You can use any bean for this Indian dish, such as lima and haricot, or substitute chickpeas. Dried pulses are an important source of protein in a vegetarian diet and, since many Indians are vegetarian, this kind of dish is very common. Of course you can also use canned dried beans, which saves a lot of time in soaking and cooking.

CURRIED DRIED BEANS

- *125 g (4 oz) dried beans*
- *1 teaspoon salt, or to taste*
- *3 teaspoons ghee or oil*
- *1 small onion, finely chopped*
- *1 clove garlic, finely chopped*
- *2 teaspoons finely chopped fresh ginger*
- *½ teaspoon ground turmeric*
- *½ teaspoon garam masala*
- *1 large ripe tomato, chopped*
- *1 fresh green chilli, seeded and chopped*
- *1 tablespoon chopped fresh mint*
- *1 tablespoon lemon juice*

Soak beans overnight in plenty of cold water to cover. Drain, rinse and put beans in a large saucepan; cover with water and add half of salt. Bring to boil, cover and simmer until tender. (If water boils away during cooking, add more.) Drain beans and reserve liquid.

Heat ghee in a saucepan and gently fry onion, garlic and

ginger until soft and golden. Add turmeric, garam masala, tomato, chilli, half of mint, lemon juice and remaining salt. Add beans and stir well over medium heat for 5 minutes. Stir in ½ cup of reserved liquid. Cover and cook over low heat until tomato and chilli are soft and sauce is thick. Stir in remaining mint and serve with rice or puris.

Potato and Pea Rissoles

- *500 g (1 lb) potatoes*
- *salt to taste*
- *1 cup fresh or frozen peas*
- *2 teaspoons ghee or oil*
- *1 small onion, finely chopped*
- *½ teaspoon finely grated fresh ginger*
- *2 tablespoons chopped fresh coriander leaves*
- *¼ teaspoon ground turmeric*
- *¼ teaspoon garam masala*
- *1 egg, beaten*
- *breadcrumbs for coating*
- *oil for deep frying*

Boil potatoes in their jackets, drain, peel and mash until smooth, adding salt to taste. Shell fresh peas or thaw frozen peas. Heat ghee or oil in a small saucepan and fry onion, ginger and coriander leaves until onion is soft and golden. Add ground spices, salt to taste and peas. (If using fresh peas, add a little water.) Cover and cook until peas are tender and liquid has evaporated. Leave to cool until lukewarm.

Divide potato into 4 portions and shape each into a flat circle. Put a spoonful of pea mixture in centre and mould smoothly to enclose. Dip each rissole in beaten egg, then in breadcrumbs. Heat oil and fry rissoles until golden brown all over. Drain on paper towel. Serve hot with Mint Chutney (see p. 79) and salad.

In India a firm, fresh cheese known as panir is used for this dish. A good substitute is baked ricotta, which is firm enough to be fried without disintegrating. It is possible to purchase baked ricotta in some Italian delicatessens, but if you have difficulty finding it, use the guidelines below to make your own.

SPINACH WITH FRESH CHEESE

- *125 g (4 oz) fresh spinach leaves, without stems*
- *250 g (8 oz) baked ricotta (see Note)*
- *oil for frying*
- *2 teaspoons ghee or oil*
- *¼ teaspoon ground turmeric*
- *¼ teaspoon kalonji (nigella) seeds*
- *2 teaspoons ground coriander*
- *¼ teaspoon chilli powder*
- *½ teaspoon finely grated fresh ginger*
- *salt to taste*
- *½ teaspoon sugar*
- *½ cup yoghurt*

Wash spinach leaves well and place with water that clings to them into a saucepan. Cover and steam until spinach wilts—this does not take long. Drain well and chop finely.

Cut ricotta into cubes. Heat oil in a small, deep frying pan and when hot, fry cubes in two lots. Drain on paper towel. Heat ghee or oil in a saucepan and add turmeric, kalonji seeds, coriander, chilli and ginger. Fry briefly, stirring constantly, being careful not to burn spices. Add spinach and salt; stir for 1 minute. Add ¼ cup hot water and sugar. Simmer for 5 minutes. Beat yoghurt until smooth and stir into spinach. Add ricotta and simmer for 10 minutes. Serve with rice.

Note To bake ricotta take 250 g (8 oz) ricotta in one block; wrap in a clean linen tea towel and leave for 1 hour so that excess moisture is absorbed. Place on a foil-lined baking tray and bake in a moderate oven for 20 minutes. Turn over with a frying slice and bake for a further 10 minutes—the cheese will be golden brown. Leave to cool and cut required amount into dice.

BEAN CURD WITH PEANUTS

- 3 cakes firm yellow bean curd
- oil for frying
- ¼ cup shelled raw peanuts
- 1 small clove garlic, crushed
- ½ teaspoon dried shrimp paste
- 3 tablespoons crunchy peanut butter
- 1 tablespoon dark soy sauce
- 1 tablespoon lemon juice
- ¼ teaspoon sambal ulek
- ½ teaspoon palm sugar or brown sugar
- 2 tablespoons canned coconut milk
- ½ cup shredded green cabbage
- ½ cup fresh bean sprouts
- 2 spring onions, finely sliced to garnish

Wipe cakes of bean curd thoroughly with paper towels. Cut into dice. Heat oil in a wok or frying pan and carefully fry bean curd until golden brown on all sides. Remove with slotted spoon and drain on paper towel. Fry peanuts in same oil for about 3 minutes. Drain and when cool, rub off skins. Set aside.

Pour off all but about 2 teaspoons of oil from pan. Fry garlic and shrimp paste over low heat, stirring constantly and crushing paste with back of a spoon. Stir in peanut butter, soy sauce, lemon juice, sambal and sugar until well mixed. Remove from heat and gradually add coconut milk and 2 tablespoons cold water until sauce is of a thick, pouring consistency.

Place fried bean curd on a serving dish. Cover with shredded cabbage and bean sprouts. Spoon sauce over and garnish with spring onions and fried peanuts.

Potato and cabbage are combined in this mildly flavoured dish, but other vegetables such as beans, cauliflower, broccoli or sweet potatoes, can be used instead.

INDONESIAN VEGETABLE CURRY

- *1 small onion, finely sliced*
- *1 small clove garlic, finely chopped*
- *1 fresh red chilli, seeded and sliced*
- *¼ teaspoon dried shrimp paste*
- *¼ teaspoon ground turmeric*
- *¾ cup canned coconut milk*
- *1 large potato, peeled and diced*
- *1½ cups coarsely shredded cabbage*
- *salt to taste*
- *lemon juice to taste*

Place onion, garlic, chilli, shrimp paste, turmeric and ¼ cup coconut milk in a saucepan. Stir in ¼ cup water and bring mixture to a simmer. Add potato and cook for 10 minutes or until half-cooked. Add cabbage and salt; cook for 3 minutes. Add remaining coconut milk and stir gently until mixture is heated through and cabbage is cooked. Remove from heat and add lemon juice and salt to taste.

STUFFED EGGPLANT

- *1 medium eggplant*
- *2 teaspoons oil*
- *1 large clove garlic, finely chopped*
- *1 small onion, finely chopped*
- *125 g (4 oz) minced pork*
- *1 medium ripe tomato, chopped*
- *salt and black pepper to taste*
- *½ cup fresh breadcrumbs*
- *1 small egg, beaten*
- *dry breadcrumbs for coating*
- *oil for frying*

Cut eggplant in halves lengthwise. Parboil in lightly salted water, remove from water and drain, cut side downwards. Scoop out some pulp, leaving sufficient to make a firm shell.

Heat oil in a pan and fry garlic and onion, stirring frequently, until golden. Add pork and fry until it is no longer pink. Stir in tomato, salt and pepper and cook for 15 minutes more. Add chopped eggplant pulp and continue cooking until most of the liquid has evaporated. Remove from heat and mix in fresh breadcrumbs, adding more seasoning if necessary.

Fill eggplant halves with mixture. Brush tops with beaten egg and sprinkle with dry breadcrumbs. Heat oil for shallow frying and fry eggplants first on one side, and then on the other, until golden. Serve hot.

BRAISED SPINACH WITH PORK

- 1 bunch fresh spinach
- 125 g (4 oz) pork fillet
- 1 tablespoon oil
- 1 clove garlic, finely chopped
- 1 tablespoon light soy sauce
- ground black pepper to taste
- 2 spring onions, finely chopped
- 1 tablespoon toasted, crushed sesame seeds

Wash spinach well, remove tough stems and break leaves into large pieces. Cut pork into very small dice. Heat oil in a wok or heavy pan and fry pork and garlic, stirring constantly, until pork changes colour. Add spinach and toss well. Season with soy sauce and pepper. Cover and simmer until spinach is tender—this will only take a short time. Add spring onions and stir well over medium heat for 2 minutes. Sprinkle with sesame seeds and serve hot.

Indian Spicy Fried Beans

- *250 g (8 oz) green beans*
- *2 teaspoons ghee or oil*
- *1 small onion, finely chopped*
- *¼ teaspoon ground turmeric*
- *¼ teaspoon chilli powder*
- *½ teaspoon garam masala*
- *salt to taste*

Trim and string beans if necessary; slice thickly. Heat ghee in a saucepan and fry onion, stirring occasionally, until golden. Add turmeric, chilli and garam masala; stir for a few seconds. Add beans and salt; cook, stirring, for about 5 minutes. Cover and cook over low heat until beans are just tender.

Spiced Potato Salad

- *250 g (8 oz) old potatoes*
- *1 tablespoon melted ghee*
- *2 tablespoons lemon juice*
- *salt to taste*
- *hot milk as required*
- *¼ cup finely chopped fresh mint leaves*
- *2 spring onions, finely chopped*

Boil or steam potatoes in their skins and as soon as they are tender, drain well, peel and mash. Add ghee, lemon juice and salt and mix in sufficient hot milk to give a smooth, creamy consistency. Taste and add more lemon juice and salt if desired—the flavour should be quite sharp. Mix in mint and spring onions. Spoon into a bowl. Serve cold or at room temperature garnished with a sprig of mint.

Serve this Thai salad as a main meal or halve the ingredients and use it as an accompaniment. It is quick to do if you have bits and pieces of cooked meats in the refrigerator . . . you can replace the crab meat with extra prawns, or with mock crab (crab sticks, crab flakes) made with fish.

WATER CHESTNUT SALAD

- 1 small can water chestnuts, drained
- 1 tablespoon oil
- 1 small onion, finely chopped
- 2 small cloves garlic, chopped
- 2 tablespoons fish sauce
- 2 tablespoons lemon juice
- 1 tablespoon sugar
- ½ cup diced cooked pork
- ½ cup chopped cooked prawns
- ½ cup cooked crab meat
- 2 tablespoons chopped fresh coriander leaves
- 2 kaffir lime leaves, finely shredded
- 2 fresh red chillies, seeded and sliced

Cut water chestnuts across into slices unless you are able to buy them already sliced.

Heat oil in a heavy pan and fry onion and garlic over medium heat—do not let them burn. Mix fish sauce, lemon juice and sugar with onions and garlic to make a dressing.

71

Combine chestnuts, pork, prawns and crab meat in a bowl and pour dressing over. Toss together. Serve garnished with chopped coriander, lime leaves and chillies.

An Indian way of cooking leeks and very tasty to serve as a vegetable accompaniment with rice.

SPICY FRIED LEEKS

- *2 large leeks*
- *2 tablespoons ghee or oil*
- *1 teaspoon cummin seeds*
- *1 teaspoon ground turmeric*
- *1 teaspoon finely grated fresh ginger*
- *1 teaspoon garam masala*
- *salt to taste*

Wash leeks well, rinsing out all grit. Cut across into fairly thick slices. Heat ghee or oil in a large saucepan and stir-fry cummin for 1 to 2 minutes. Add turmeric and ginger; fry for 1 minute more. Add leeks and stir well into mixture; fry for 5 minutes. Sprinkle with garam masala and salt. Cover and cook until tender, stirring occasionally.

For this unusual Thai salad try to use old-fashioned roses which have a lovely fragrance. Whether from your garden or a shop, make sure they have not been sprayed with pesticides. Vary the meats and seafood in this salad according to your own taste. You will find crisp, fried garlic and shallots in Asian food stores.

Rose Petal Salad

- 2 full-blown roses
- 1 cooked chicken breast fillet
- ½ cup small cooked prawns
- ½ cup shredded cooked pork
- 6 pink grapefruit segments
- 2 tablespoons crushed roasted peanuts
- 1 teaspoon crisply fried garlic
- 2 teaspoons crisply fried shallots
- few leaves of frilled lettuce
- cucumber slices
- 1 tablespoon fish sauce
- 1 teaspoon sugar
- 2 teaspoons lime juice
- ½ fresh red chilli, seeded and finely sliced

Carefully wash roses with cold water; shake gently and place on paper towels to drain, petals downwards. Cut chicken meat into thin strips; shell and devein prawns.

In a bowl mix chicken, prawns, pork, grapefruit segments,

1 tablespoon of peanuts, fried garlic and shallots. Arrange over lettuce leaves on individual plates. Garnish with cucumber slices.

In a small bowl stir fish sauce, sugar, lime juice and chilli until sugar dissolves. Spoon mixture over combined ingredients. Remove petals from roses and scatter over the top. Sprinkle with remaining peanuts.

An interesting feature of Asian food is the combination of fruit and salty, hot flavours.

INDONESIAN SPICY FRUIT SALAD

- *1 small grapefruit*
- *1 small orange or mandarin*
- *1 small seedless cucumber*
- *½ small pineapple*
- *¼ teaspoon dried shrimp paste*
- *1 teaspoon sambal ulek*
- *2 teaspoons palm sugar or brown sugar*
- *2 teaspoons dark soy sauce*
- *1 tablespoon lemon juice*

Peel grapefruit and orange or mandarin, removing white pith. Peel segments, discard seeds. Place in a bowl. Wash cucumber, cut into quarters lengthwise and then slice these strips across into small wedges.

Peel pineapple and remove core. Slice, then cut into small wedges. Add cucumber and pineapple to bowl.

Stir shrimp paste, sambal ulek and sugar into soy sauce and lemon juice until dissolved. Pour over fruit and mix well. Let stand for a few minutes before serving.

Accompaniments

This relish is meant to be hot, but if preferred reduce the heat by removing the seeds from the chillies and by reducing the number of chillies.

Onion and Tamarind Relish

- *1 medium onion, finely sliced*
- *salt to taste*
- *1 teaspoon tamarind pulp*
- *1 tablespoon palm sugar or brown sugar*
- *1 firm ripe tomato, diced*
- *2 teaspoons fine shreds of fresh ginger*
- *2 fresh red or green chillies, sliced*
- *1 tablespoon chopped fresh coriander leaves*

Sprinkle onion generously with salt and leave for 1 hour. Press out all liquid and rinse once with cold water. Drain. Soak tamarind pulp in 2 tablespoons hot water for about 2 minutes. Squeeze to dissolve pulp in water. Strain, adding a little more water if liquid is too thick. Stir sugar into tamarind liquid until dissolved. Mix all ingredients together in a bowl, adding extra salt to taste if desired. Chill before serving.

BITTER MELON SAMBOL

- *1 bitter melon*
- *½ teaspoon ground turmeric*
- *½ teaspoon salt*
- *oil for shallow frying*
- *1 small onion, very thinly sliced*
- *1 fresh green chilli, seeded and sliced*
- *lemon juice to taste*

Wash melon and cut across into thin slices. Rub with turmeric and salt and fry in oil until golden brown, turning to cook both sides. Drain on paper towel, then mix with onion and chilli. Season with lemon juice and add more salt if necessary.

Cucumber with Yoghurt

- 1 medium green cucumber
- 1 teaspoon salt
- 1 small clove garlic, crushed
- ¼ teaspoon finely grated fresh ginger
- ½ cup yoghurt
- lemon juice to taste

Peel cucumber; cut in half lengthwise and scoop out seeds with a teaspoon. Slice each half across thinly. Put into a bowl, sprinkle with salt and chill for 1 hour. Pour off liquid from cucumbers, pressing out as much as possible. Mix garlic and ginger with yoghurt; stir in with cucumbers, combining thoroughly. Add lemon juice and more salt to taste if necessary.

The coconut milk in this recipe is intended as a dressing for the cucumber and is used rich and undiluted, straight from the can.

Cucumber Salad

- 1 small green cucumber
- 1 teaspoon salt
- ¼ cup canned coconut milk
- 1 fresh red chilli, seeded and sliced
- 1 small onion, sliced very thinly
- 1 tablespoon lemon juice

Peel cucumber and slice thinly. Place in a bowl, sprinkle with salt and set aside for 30 minutes. Press out all liquid and if you wish to remove salt rinse with cold water, squeeze out excess. Mix in a bowl with remaining ingredients, chill and serve as an accompaniment to a curry.

TOMATO AND MINT SALAD

- 2 firm red tomatoes
- 3 spring onions
- ¼ cup fresh mint leaves
- 2 tablespoons lemon juice
- salt to taste
- ¼ teaspoon chilli powder
- 1 teaspoon sugar

Dice tomatoes fairly small. Slice spring onions and chop mint leaves. Mix lemon juice, salt and chilli powder in a serving bowl; stir in sugar until it dissolves. Add tomatoes, spring onions and mint and toss lightly but thoroughly. Cover and chill until serving time.

Fresh Mint Chutney

- ½ cup fresh mint leaves
- 2 spring onions, roughly chopped
- 1 small green chilli, seeds removed
- 1 small clove garlic
- juice of ½ lemon
- 1 teaspoon sugar
- salt to taste
- ½ teaspoon garam masala
- 1 tablespoon cold water

Place all ingredients in the container of an electric blender and blend to a smooth purée, scraping down side of container from time to time. Serve in a small bowl.

Variation Add 2 tablespoons grated fresh coconut or desiccated coconut when blending. Stir 3 tablespoons unflavoured yoghurt into blended mixture.

Coconut Sambol

- ½ cup fresh grated or desiccated coconut
- ½ teaspoon salt
- ½ teaspoon chilli powder
- 1 teaspoon paprika
- 1 teaspoon dried prawn powder, optional
- 1 tablespoon lemon juice
- 1 small onion, finely chopped
- 1 fresh green chilli, seeded and finely chopped
- 1 to 2 tablespoons hot milk

Mix together coconut, salt, chilli powder, paprika and prawn powder in a bowl. Sprinkle with lemon juice, onion, green chilli and milk. Mix well, rubbing together with your fingers so that the coconut is moistened evenly. Mound into a small bowl.

Green Bean Sambal

- 125 g (4 oz) fresh green beans
- 2 teaspoons peanut oil
- ½ teaspoon crushed garlic
- ¼ teaspoon sambal ulek
- salt to taste
- 1 spring onion, finely sliced

Trim beans, remove strings if necessary and cut across in fine diagonal slices. Heat oil in a wok or heavy frying pan and toss beans over high heat for 2 minutes. Add garlic and fry 1 minute more. Stir in sambal and salt and cook 1 minute longer. Beans should be tender but still crisp. Remove from heat and mix in spring onion slices. Serve with curry and rice.

A dry relish to serve with rice and curry.

SPICED COCONUT WITH PEANUTS

- *½ cup desiccated coconut*
- *2 tablespoons dried onion flakes*
- *½ teaspoon instant minced garlic*
- *½ teaspoon ground coriander*
- *½ teaspoon ground cummin*
- *salt to taste*
- *½ cup roasted unsalted peanuts*

In a dry frying pan toast coconut over medium low heat, stirring until golden. Crush onion flakes into small pieces. Add with garlic to frying pan. Continue to stir mixture over heat until coconut turns a deep golden and garlic and onion are toasted. Add coriander, cummin and salt. Stir well, then remove from heat. Allow to cool, add peanuts. This will keep for some weeks stored in a bottle.

PAPPADAMS (SPICED LENTIL WAFERS)

These are purchased dried in packets. You need only deep-fry them for a few seconds in hot oil. The oil should be hot enough for the pappadams to swell and double in size as soon as they are dropped in. Turn over with tongs and remove as soon as they are a pale golden colour. Cook only one at a time and drain on paper towel. If you have to make them a few hours ahead, store in an airtight container once they are cool. Pappadams can also be cooked under a grill—watch carefully so they don't burn—or in a microwave. Microwave 2 large or 4 small pappadams on High for 50 to 55 seconds, turning them around after 30 seconds.

VEGETABLE PICKLE

- *1 cup carrot sticks*
- *1 cup green beans*
- *10 fresh red and green chillies*
- *2 small green seedless cucumbers*
- *2 tablespoons peanut oil*
- *2 cloves garlic, finely grated*
- *2 teaspoons finely grated fresh ginger*
- *1 teaspoon ground turmeric*
- *½ cup white vinegar*
- *2 teaspoons sugar*
- *1 teaspoon salt*
- *1 cup cauliflower sprigs*

Cut carrots into julienne strips. Cut beans into pieces of same length and slice in two lengthwise unless beans are very young and narrow. Remove stems from chillies. Wash cucumbers. Slice in half lengthwise and then cut into strips similar to carrots.

Heat oil in a saucepan and fry garlic and ginger over low heat for 1 minute. Stir in turmeric. Add vinegar, sugar and salt with ½ cup water and bring to boil. Add carrots, beans, chillies and cauliflower sprigs. Return to boil and cook for 3 minutes. Add cucumber and boil for 1 more minute. Transfer to an earthenware or glass bowl and allow to cool. The pickle can be used immediately or bottle and refrigerate.

This tasty Sri Lankan accompaniment should have a fairly dry consistency. Serve with curries and rice.

Shredded Radish Leaf Salad

- *Leaves from half a bunch of small red radishes*
- *1 small onion, finely chopped*
- *¼ teaspoon ground turmeric*
- *1 teaspoon dried prawn powder*
- *2 teaspoons lemon juice*
- *¼ teaspoon salt*
- *⅛ teaspoon chilli powder*
- *1 tablespoon desiccated coconut*

Wash radish leaves well, discarding any that are yellow or withered. Chop finely and put into a saucepan with the water that clings to the leaves and remaining ingredients except coconut. Cover and cook over medium heat. The leaves will wilt as their moisture evaporates.

When mixture is almost dry add coconut and stir over low heat for about 3 minutes or until coconut has absorbed any remaining liquid.

This Thai salad has a distinctive smoky flavour which comes from charring the skin of the eggplants.

ROASTED EGGPLANT SALAD

- 2 slender eggplants
- 1 small clove garlic
- 1 teaspoon sugar
- salt to taste
- 1 tablespoon fresh lime juice
- 2 teaspoons fish sauce
- 2 tablespoons dried shrimp
- few slices of red chilli
- fresh coriander sprigs

Wash and dry eggplants. Prick well and cut off stem ends. Cut in halves lengthwise and char under a griller. Set aside and when cool enough to handle, carefully remove all skin. Place on a serving dish.

Crush garlic with sugar and salt. Add lime juice and fish sauce and stir to dissolve sugar. Taste dressing—it should be a combination of sweet, sour and salty. Spoon over eggplants.

Remove any dark spots from dried shrimp. Place shrimp in a blender or food processor and reduce to a floss. Sprinkle over eggplants. Scatter with chilli slices and fresh coriander. Serve at room temperature.

GLOSSARY

You can find most of these ingredients in Asian food stores, but many are also sold in supermarkets, etc.

BEAN CURD   Made from soy beans and high in protein. Available in various forms—soft, firm, fried or tetra packs.

BLACK BEANS   Salted, fermented soy beans, sold canned or packeted.

CHILLI BEAN SAUCE   Sold in jars. It is very hot and should be used with discretion.

CHILLIES   Handle with care as the volatile oils can cause discomfort to the eyes and skin. Wear gloves, especially when chopping. Buy chopped chillies in jars or sambal ulek, a mixture of fresh chillies and salt. Soak dried chillies before using. Small chillies are hotter than large ones.

COCONUT MILK   Some brands of canned coconut milk are very thick and rich, others extremely thin. Dilute the former with water in equal parts; use the latter straight from the can.

CORIANDER   Coriander seeds and fresh coriander are different in flavour and usage. Dried ground coriander seeds are one of the main ingredients in curries. Fresh coriander herb is an essential ingredient in Thai and Chinese cooking.

CURRY LEAVES (MURRAYA KOENIGII)   Usually sold dried, but some shops sell fresh curry leaves or you can grow the plant itself.

FISH SAUCE   A thin, salty sauce used in South-East Asian food.

FIVE SPICE POWDER   Popular in Chinese cooking—ground star anise, fennel, cinnamon, cloves and Szechwan pepper.

GALANGAL (ALPINIA GALANGA)   Also known as laos or lengkuas. Similar in size and appearance to ginger. Can be bought pickled in brine, which keeps indefinitely in the refrigerator. Also sold as dried slices or powder.

GARAM MASALA   Essential in Indian dishes. Roast separately until fragrant 2 tablespoons coriander seeds, 1 tablespoon cummin seeds, 2 teaspoons whole black peppercorns, 1 teaspoon cardamon seeds (remove from pods), 2 cinnamon sticks and 10 whole cloves. Grind as finely as possible and mix in half a nutmeg, finely grated. Store airtight.

GINGER   Fresh ginger root is sold at most greengrocers. Dried ground ginger is no substitute.

KAFFIR LIME LEAVES   Essential in Thai cooking. Sold fresh, frozen and dried.

KALONJI SEEDS (NIGELLA)   Sometimes called black cummin, although not a member of the cummin family. There is no substitute. Sold mostly in Indian shops.

LAOS   *See* **Galangal**.

LEMON GRASS   Grows easily in Australia. Use the white or pale green portion of the stem, which is tender enough to slice finely. Substitute with 2 strips thinly peeled lemon rind for each stem of lemon grass.

MAGGI SAUCE   A flavouring which the manufacturers claim contains no added monosodium glutamate. It is given here as a substitute for Golden Mountain Sauce which is similar but contains MSG.

MUSHROOMS   Dried Chinese or Japanese mushrooms are the shiitake variety. Dried European mushrooms are no substitute.

OYSTER SAUCE   A thick sauce used in Chinese food.

PALM SUGAR   Has a distinct flavour but can be substituted with brown sugar.

PRAWN POWDER   Gives flavour to many South-East Asian dishes. Can be purchased ground, or you can make it yourself by grinding dried shrimp (sold in packets) in a blender

RICE Try to obtain the delicately perfumed, long grain varieties basmati or jasmine because they are very special.

ROTI FLOUR Also called Sharps, the term used by millers, which denotes the grade to which it is milled. Slightly granular, it is similar to continental flour which can be substituted.

SAFFRON Try to get true saffron because there are many imitations and nothing else has the same flavour. Expensive, but very little is needed and it keeps well if stored airtight. Made from the dried stigmas of the saffron crocus, it is sold in strands (best to buy these) or tiny packets of powder. Distrust cheap saffron—there is no such thing.

SAMBAL ULEK (OELEK) *See* **Chillies**.

SESAME OIL Use oriental sesame oil made from roasted sesame, which is dark in colour and very aromatic.

SHRIMP PASTE Made from dried shrimp, this is used in tiny quantities and is a mainstay of South-East Asian cuisines. Sold in jars or blocks. Keeps indefinitely.

SOY SAUCE You need dark soy (thick, coloured with caramel); light soy (thin, saltier than dark); and Japanese soy (shoyu). For best results, use the specified kind.

STAR ANISE Dried, star-shaped seed pod for flavouring in Chinese food. Simmered in long-cooked dishes.

SZECHWAN PEPPER Small dried berries that are not hot in the conventional sense, but leave a numbing sensation on the tongue. Only the brown husks provide flavour. Roast over low heat to make them aromatic and crush to powder.

TAMARIND Gives acidity to many dishes. It is sold dried, puréed or instant. The dried pulp has the truest flavour.

TURMERIC The rhizome is dried and ground to a yellow powder and is used to flavour and colour rice and curries.

INDEX